THE TIDE HAS TURNED

*What Will Become of the church in
Britain and the West?*

ANTHONY WHELAN

TONY WHELAN MEDIA

Cover design:
Tony Whelan Media.

ISBN 978-1-0687441-0-5

Contents

Little Boy Blue,
Come blow your horn,
The sheep's in the meadow,
The cow's in the corn.
Where's the boy
Who looks after the sheep?
He's under the haystack,
Fast asleep.
Will you wake him?
No, not I,
For if I do,
He's sure to cry.

Anon.
Old English Nursery Rhyme.

ACKNOWLEDGEMENTS

I would like to thank Kathryn for her expert readings and critique. I am grateful to Dr Clifford Denton for his extensive knowledge on the topics covered and his thorough review and feedback on the manuscript. I also appreciate the assistance of another Phd, who wishes to remain anonymous, for their critiques and comments. Lastly, I want to express my gratitude to Monica (not related to Dr Denton) for her insightful comments.

PROLOGUE

The Tide Has Turned

Summer 1962, Southend-on-Sea, Essex, the school holidays. My journey to the beach with school friends Rob and Harvey took about forty-five minutes. We walked down from the council estates of the seaside town.

Upon reaching the beach, we noticed the tide had been going out for a while. The sweltering heat urged us to swim, and our attention turned to following the receding water across the mud flats and out into the Thames Estuary.

"Let's go out to The Ray," I suggested.

Rob quickly agreed, and after some persuasion, Harvey reluctantly joined us.

We scoured the bustling promenade for a spot to change and leave our belongings. We found some upturned rowing boats on a concrete slope above the beach, we stripped down to our shorts, stashed our gear in backpacks, and set out for The Ray. We walked barefoot to avoid the sticky, shoe-swallowing mud. Harvey grumbled about the sludge. As we made our way, we ignored the warning sign on the beach about tides, as we considered ourselves experienced with these waters.

The Ray, as we called it, was a vast sandbank raised a few metres above the surrounding mud flats. Later, as adults, we will discover that The Ray is not actually the sandbank but the deep, wide, stream cut into the seabed in front of it. The stream was moving sluggishly from West to East, that is, from London out to sea. The water of the receding tide didn't reach my knees as I crossed. The bottom of the creek was lower than the mud flats and well below the height of the sandbank. I stood in the middle of the creek and looked up, impressed with its height. It is about a mile in length, a quarter of a mile wide and a significant distance from the beach. As we climbed onto the sandbank, we were relieved to feel firm, smooth sand underfoot, a welcome contrast to the sharp shells and stones we had encountered in the mud.

Exhilaration overcame us. Jumping, dancing, and running along the water's edge. We even raced to the other side, closer to the deeper waters, where sailing boats and motor launches glided. Further out in the estuary a cargo ship passed by en route to the London docks, grey smoke billowed from its funnel.

Rob produced a tennis ball, and we played catch. Then, I had an idea.

"I'm going to make a marker," I shouted, as I ran back to where we crossed the stream. I scooped up some of the silt and made three small mounds as markers to check the tide. Striding down the slope from the markers to the water I counted eight steps. I ran back to my friends.

We played catch or ran and splashed in the water. Other groups of children or families were doing the same; they called out to each other, throwing beach balls, and squealing with delight. The openness of the landscape and the sky together with the warm sunlight was making us glad. Our games continued for over an hour. However, the atmosphere changed suddenly. The sun disappeared behind a cloud, a chilly breeze swept over the estuary, and the once crowded sandbank fell eerily silent.

We noticed that we were alone, save for two small groups of people just reaching the other side of the creek where we had crossed earlier. Panic set in as we realised the tide had turned, and we needed to get off the sandbank immediately. We sprinted back across the plateau, trying to locate my markers, but they were gone. We dashed down the slope into the creek.

Rob and I could swim but weren't strong swimmers, and Harvey couldn't swim at all. We hesitated to enter the water as the current was too powerful. The current was running the opposite way much faster and more powerful. The creek had become deeper, wider, and the tide was rising swiftly. If we ventured further, we risked being swept away by the strong current. Desperation took hold as we watched another man further up the creek being carried downstream. We tried to wave and shout to him for help, but he couldn't hear us. He thought we were waving for fun.

Fear and panic intensified as we became aware of the grim situation. Shivering with cold, we understood that we were stranded. Harvey's face was becoming twisted out of shape. I'd never seen him like this. His forehead was furrowed, and his eyes were filling up with tears. They started to roll down his face. I saw the fear in him, and it increased mine. We saw the fear in each other. We kept moving higher up the bank as the tide surged in.

We waved frantically at people on the beach but it's too far away. We continued to wave and scream for help, but the man across the mudflats had all but disappeared from sight.

Our attention was so focussed on looking for him, we didn't see what was happening behind us.

A small boat had appeared, piloted by an elderly couple. They looked ancient to my young eyes but were probably only middle-aged. The boat was being carried silently along on the swift current. They landed the boat on the edge of the sandbank, signalling for us to board. They didn't utter a word, but their smiles conveyed their understanding of our predicament. Our relief was palpable. They started the outboard motor, and we crossed to the other side of the creek. We disembarked with heartfelt thanks and watched as they piloted their boat back into the incoming tide and then up the creek towards Leigh-on-Sea.

As we returned to the beach, still shaken by our ordeal, Harvey wondered, "Do they spend the whole summer rescuing people on The Ray?"

Our thoughts lingered on the terrifying possibilities of what might have happened that day. However, we were profoundly grateful for our rescuers and getting back to the safety of the beach. The sun had reappeared. We laid our towels on the sand, basking in its warmth, thankful for our miraculous escape.

An Explanation

The real-life story above serves as an allegory for the predicament of many people across the globe. People worldwide have fallen victim to deceptive ideologies, and surprisingly, a significant portion of the Church in the Western world is in a similar situation. You might expect the world to be deceived, given that it is under the rule of the evil one (see 1 John 5:19), but can you contemplate that the Church is also ensnared by various deceptions?

These deceptions come from external and internal sources and can include anything from political ideologies to divergent interpretations of biblical teachings. In this book, and connected studies I have made, I try to unravel these by investigating them and revealing their roots.

The carefree children on the sandbank symbolise a significant portion of the Church today. They are on a sandbank that offers an idealised vision of the Church and its future, but this is a mirage. The children and their leaders will eventually confront reality. They failed to check the tide times or heed warning signs. They either believed they comprehended the dangers or were oblivious to them, leaving them in a perilous state.

The incoming tide, and the threat it poses, is a collection of fuzzy, unexamined beliefs that will become increasingly menacing for believers. Today, many church leaders and believers have not diligently studied their Bibles or tried to understand the times in which we are living, something Jesus explicitly advised (see Matthew 24 and Luke 21).

Imagine if an adult, say a teacher, as part of a nature walk, had led a group of school pupils onto that sandbank without alerting them to the impending tide. The teacher might have falsely reassured them or, even worse, remained silent. This is neglect, and it is what is happening in many churches. Leaders are not necessarily deliberately leading people into danger but are deluded due to their belief systems.

Delusions, fantasies—they all share one commonality: they lack truth. The realisation that leaders in some churches had fallen prey to various delusions was not easy to accept, but it became a contemplation that started in 2017. This initiated a journey of discovery, during which I began collecting information, making notes, and seeking God's guidance regarding the things I was uncovering. This book tells of my discoveries and the conclusions I reached about the Church and its position in the world.

My discoveries aren't novel or exclusive revelations. They merely represent a clear understanding of what God's Word has already conveyed. My intention is for readers to gain insight into contemporary global affairs through the truth found in God's Word. Discovering this truth, and relinquishing any worries that arise because of it, can bring lasting peace (see Philippians 4:6). There has been false teaching, lack of discernment, deception, and neglect, but I hope this book and its recommendations serve as a rescue vessel.

My research is limited and fallible, but I've done my utmost to provide you with a solid starting point. The explanation of the sandbank allegory, talk of deception, delusion, and fantasy may initially appear extraordinary, but these things will become clear as you read on.

INTRODUCTION

In the year that Queen Elizabeth died, I completed the initial draft of this book. I began compiling it several years before. This was after God disturbed an unhealthy indifference to truth I had succumbed to.

My motivation is to share a sense of urgency with my fellow Christians. I aim to forewarn you about the impending challenges facing both the nation and the Western Church in these last days. My particular concern is the younger generations in our churches, who are being taught erroneous beliefs that may leave them unprepared for the trials ahead.

We are going to see some previously presumed vibrant churches, denominations, and church streams, come down in smoke and ash. I mean this mostly in the metaphorical sense but, sadly, in some instances, it will be literal.

But, of course, the metaphor that more tellingly illustrates the threat facing the churches of the UK and the West is that of a creeping tide which has gone unnoticed my many.

If you are alive, if you are spiritually awake, if you are watching, and praying about what is going on in the world, then you will be aware that in the last few years a change has clearly taken place.

This is not something entirely new but rather the rapid progression of a shift that became noticeable around 70 years ago. By examining it, we can identify signs that demand our attention. This story is not a game of kiss and tell. It is an urgently required proclamation of truths that have been subverted by shoddy and dubious teaching in some churches over many decades.

The implications of this, as you will see, are momentous.

My intention is not to preach but to come alongside you, sharing how I unearthed essential insights about the perplexing and perilous times we are living in.

How to read this book

I recount various aspects of my journey in different styles. In some instances, I provide a straightforward memoir-style account of lived experiences, recounting events as they occurred without subjective reflection on whether they were right or wrong. This approach mirrors my initial experiences when I lacked an understanding of their underlying significance.

Some stories should be told exactly as they happened, preserving their tragic, beautiful, or ugly reality.

There is no way of telling this story without telling my own. I write about things I witnessed and participated in, often with a degree of naivety. Upon revisiting these events I reflect on them with a more critical eye. These experiences formed part of God's work in my life, guiding me to my present understanding.

I use allegory, moral tales, and contemporary parables to deepen readers' understanding of my observations. Through academic research, investigative journalism, and reportage, I present a reliable account of the events I have witnessed. While some parts may resemble biblical teaching, my aim is simply to tell a story about the things I have discovered. These elements remain ongoing.

I have not always displayed Bible verses in full because I want readers to search and find the scriptures for themselves. I also suggest that, while doing this, readers should examine the context in which those scriptures are written.

The Joy Set Before Us

Many remarkable events are on the horizon. Some will be remarkable due to their sheer horror, but they will ultimately pale in comparison to the extraordinary experiences awaiting believers afterward.

We are entering an era of great distress and perplexity

among the nations of the world referred to in the Bible as the tribulation and the great tribulation. Jesus predicted that the world would face unprecedented challenges, and we should prepare accordingly.

That's the near future, but the long-term prospects for genuine followers of Jesus are glorious. Despite the perilous times ahead, our ultimate destination is a focus of great hope.

On Sleeping

Paul said we need to understand the present time:

"the hour has come for you to wake up from your slumber, because our salvation is nearer now than when we first believed. The night is nearly over; the day is almost here" (Romans 13:11, 12a).

Some characteristics of sleep include not realising you are asleep until you wake, engaging in actions you wouldn't when awake, and ... despising the sound of an alarm.

While some churches and church streams may appear awake by their actions, such as planting new churches and engaging in social activities, they often operate in a bubble, oblivious to world events and God's plan. In some cases, there are delusions about what the Church can achieve during this age, which urgently need correction.

Before delving into this, I'd like to introduce myself and my background to establish a foundation for the forthcoming content.

Chapter 1

WHERE I WAS FROM

A Sense of Place

I was born in Southend, Essex. The town had been a revered seaside resort, frequented by royalty, during the Edwardian and Victorian eras. The introduction of the railway in the mid-1800s and the subsequent influx of seaside day-trippers bolstered Southend's popularity, leading to rapid expansion into a bustling town. Its proximity to London made it a favoured destination for visitors seeking day trips, weekends, or longer stays. In the early 1900s, numerous bed and break-fast establishments and small hotels emerged along or near the seafront, accompanied by a proliferation of public houses.

By the mid-1900s, a string of seafront pubs, amusement arcades, and nightclubs earned the town a reputation for revelry. Swarms of Londoners, predominantly from the East End, would inundate the bars and taverns during their brief stays throughout the summer seasons. They arrived by trains or in convoys of buses, which would spend one night or several parked in a vast coach park behind The Kursaal, an amusement and music venue located on the seafront.

However, with the rise of foreign travel, the number of visitors dwindled, and many once-popular venues began to fall into disrepair. As the population increasingly opted for holidays abroad, the traditional British pastime of seaside vacations became outdated. Consequently, the town fell into a state of fatigue and neglect. Like most towns, there are good and bad parts, but the run-down part was the Southend I remember. The Southend I grew up in.

Family Life

I was part of a family of Irish Catholics, the youngest of ten children—seven boys and three girls. My father left around the time I was born. I never knew him. He visited our home a few times during my early years, and I had to ask my mother who the strange visitor was.

My mother was there in body but not in spirit. Her alcoholism left me with a mother I also never knew. As I grew, I found it hard to conjure memories of her any other way.

Religion and superstition were bound up with the church attendance imposed on us. The Catholic school was on the same site as the church building. We would often go from lessons in a school classroom to lessons, usually on Religious Education, in the church building. My sisters went to a Catholic Convent school a few miles away. Their tales were rife with the harsh treatment meted out by the nuns who were supposed to be teaching them.

During my formative years, my siblings, except for the four youngest, donned the uniforms of the Armed Forces. They were often away for long periods of time stationed in various trouble spots around the globe. As they returned to civilian life, the sanctuary of home proved a fleeting refuge before they scattered to find their own havens elsewhere. Dysfunctional home and family life led my siblings to go off the rails, living in rooms and flats around the town exploring freedoms they weren't prepared for.

The post-war era brought economic prosperity, ample job opportunities, and companies eager to train their employees. My sisters learned skills like typing and using early office computers. The older siblings sought comfort in local pubs and clubs, yearning for love, stable homes, and families of their own, hoping to escape the troubles of our home life, characterised by abuse and neglect.

I discovered my own way to escape the unease; I lost myself in a world of books like *Gulliver's Travels*, *Moby-Dick*, *Robinson Crusoe*, *The Scarlet Pimpernel*, *The Count of Monte Cristo*, Hans

Christian Anderson's tales, many kinds of comics, stories of war heroes and great explorers. These narratives typically revolved around a courageous protagonist, a conflict of good versus evil, and a principled resolution.

Losing My Religion

Society was increasingly sceptical of religion, which was predominantly Christian at the time. Conversations about God often questioned His benevolence, considering the death and suffering brought by the war. People, especially the younger generations, drifted away from traditional Christian beliefs and questioned the sanctity of marriage.

The younger generations led in this but the older generations, for the most part, agreed with them. They did not have much fight left to disagree and if you did disagree then you were regarded as old-fashioned and bigoted. Marriage, once a sacred institution, now bore the brunt of scepticism. It was said that marriage amounted to nothing more than "just a piece of paper" and "living in sin" – a term for cohabiting – was used as a flippant way of mocking the old attitudes toward right and wrong.

From 1956 to 1960, I attended a boy's boarding school in Kent. I wasn't sent there to get a good or better education. The school was like an orphanage and had been established to provide a refuge for boys whose lives had been marred by wartime bereavement or hardship, a place borne out of noble ideals in the late 1800s, with patrons like King George V, Queen Mary, and Field Marshal Montgomery gracing its history.

By the time I got there, the school's noble origins had dimmed and treatment of the boys, if it had ever been reasonable, left much to be desired and was, at times, brutal. On the surface, it might have seemed an idyllic setting, a place for young boys to grow and learn trades, but like so many other institutions, it was marred by the scourge of bullying, physical, mental, and even sexual abuse.

Yet there were periods of relief; the summer holidays

provided a temporary escape for most children as they returned to their families. For the few of us without such arrangements, there was an unexpected adventure in store–days spent in orphanages and other large rambling homes in seaside towns around the Kent coast, day trips to Biggin Hill Air Show or Brands Hatch motor racing.

The standard of education offered was far from exemplary, and when I eventually returned to a junior school in Southend for my last year, the crucial 11-Plus exam proved an insurmountable hurdle. When the time came for me to progress to secondary school, my mother, disillusioned with the Catholic Church, laid a choice before me: continue attending the Catholic school or switch to the local state school. All the friends in my street were part of the latter, and so my decision was made.

At home, raucous parties often punctuated weekends when siblings were home from their stints in the Armed Forces, or if there was a birthday. Surrounded by revelry and clinking glasses, I became curious about the tantalising drinks on offer, and was often granted a sip or two. My older brothers and their pals found it amusing to watch the little lad trying to keep up.

Up to that age, I spent extended periods at my grandmother's home in Westcliff, a few miles away. I never questioned why I was taken there. I never knew what my mother was doing or why I couldn't stay at home. Adults arranged the lives of children and usually it was fruitless to question things. My grandmother's house was a sanctuary of sorts because, though sombre in its Victorian decor, it offered a less intimidating environment.

Over the next few years life took a turn for the worse. The winter of 1962-1963 was the coldest on record in England for over 200 years. There were blizzards and deep snow drifts everywhere in what became known as "The Big Freeze." The newspapers showed pictures of the Thames frozen over in places and there was fear that ice might damage the supports of Southend Pier. My grandmother died in January and over the ensuing ten months, my mother's health declined steadily until she was eventually hospitalised. In 1964, she died of liver failure, leaving me grappling with the profound mysteries of mortality. The unspoken questions hung heavy in the air. Why must people die? Silence surrounded the topic, and it seemed inappropriate to probe. I had stumbled upon a harsh tutor named Experience, who offered no gentle lessons.

After my mother died, I went to stay with my eldest sister, newly married and living on Canvey Island. This didn't last, as she soon became pregnant, and the circumstances required my departure. I then went to live with my eldest brother while arrangements were made for my placement into care in the nearby town of Hadleigh. It was 1965 and my schooling was coming to an end so, I clung to the expectation that life would improve once I had left.

Life after school failed to blossom as I had hoped. Sometimes I was living back at my brother's house and sometimes I was asked to leave because I was unemployed and not contributing to the household budget. A moment of optimism arrived when I started a Diploma Course at the Southend College of Art and Design, but this was short-lived as the family could not afford to support this venture.

My teens and twenties were an unpredictable time and, although there were seasons of progress, the general direction of my life was downward.

Inside and Out

I experienced times of homelessness, heavy drinking, drug-taking, relationships with various women, police arrests and, at one point, two years in prison. When I say prison, I mean what would now be called a young offenders institute.

A serious or repeated offence would lead to a spell in a Detention Centre which was highly regulated and very strict. It was part of a government plan to reduce the rapidly increasing youth crime rate by giving offenders a "short, sharp, shock".

Less serious offences, like mine, meant you were sent to Borstal which could be "open" or "closed" depending on the severity of your crime. While being allocated to a Borstal appropriate to my offences (mostly burglary) I had to undergo psychological tests and intelligence assessments. These were held at various centres in the main prisons of the UK. This procedure required most young offenders to be transferred across the country in stages, moving from one prison to another until they reached the establishment deemed most suitable for their punishment and rehabilitation. At the time of my arrest, I was living in the north of England, so I began my journey there. I spent time in most of the country's major prisons: Armley Jail in Leeds, Walton Prison in Liverpool, Strangeways in Manchester, quite a long time in Wormwood Scrubs in London and a few other prisons along the way.

I will not go into detail about how I learned to survive in such places; it was a hard time; the substance abuse, the rapes, and the suicides. I will simply say that it was a salutary lesson and I determined to never do anything in future that would lead to me going back "inside".

When I got out, I miraculously secured a position in a printing firm. The company owner's brother, a probation officer, had pulled some strings to give me a chance of rehabilitation. The transition from the sheltered cocoon of prison to the unruly pandemonium of society proved quite a shock.

The late 1960s was a time of rampant drug use, civil unrest, and a sexual awakening so profound it would have made the Victorians faint. All of this was underpinned by the influences of the counterculture and the ensuing student protest movement being imported from America.

Ah, satire, the British way of showing contempt and defiance toward those in authority. We gleefully joined in the national pastime of ridiculing them through TV programs like That Was the Week That Was and the zany antics of Monty Python's Flying Circus.

Civil disobedience was common, and the drug culture was a part of this. Most of my friends were swept along by these societal shifts viewing them as a kind of evolutionary process. The rampant use of hallucinogenic drugs, particularly LSD[1], promised to "open up your mind" to fresh ideas.

A popular song of the era summed up the changing times, encouraging young people to embrace a new way of life, one brimming with goodwill and kindness toward others. This song, written to promote a Pop Festival[2], emerged from an America deeply embroiled in the Vietnam War and threats of nuclear devastation from the Cold War, as if to say, "Why not have a party while the world goes up in smoke?"

The Right Stuff?

In those days, most of my friends were as familiar with drugs as they were with fish and chips. Amphetamines of various sorts were favoured as "uppers," while sleeping pills and antidepressants were the choice "downers." These were often prescription medications, stolen from chemist shops or supplied through the services of "Doctor Feelgood," a physician with a rather flexible prescription pad. They were all used together with the ubiquitous cannabis resin.

As an introduction to the whole weekends' activities, Friday evenings saw a motley crew of friends gathering at someone's flat to partake in the ritual of injecting Methedrine, a liquid methamphetamine, or heroin. These substances, pure as the driven snow, were, you guessed it, procured through unconventional means, courtesy of the friendly neighbourhood chemist or a daring pharmaceutical heist. Our method of choice was "skin-popping," an act reminiscent of receiving a school vaccination, an irony not lost on us. Injecting intravenously, or "mainlining," was frowned upon, as it was believed to be the express lane to addiction.

Drug-taking became a form of communal therapy. It offered both camaraderie and a sense of belonging, not only with each other but also with the world of pop and rock musicians who embraced and sang about their own chemical adventures. We understood a different meaning behind the Beatles' lyrics, realising that 'the movement we needed on the shoulder' was a shot in the arm that could indeed 'make things better', temporarily anyway. Of course, when pressed to explain their song lyrics in public, the Beatles employed a bit of slapstick, spinning tales far removed from the realities of drug use. *Lucy in the Sky with Diamonds* (LSD) and *(I get by) with a Little Help from My Friends* were some examples.

As the 1970s rolled in, increased security measures put a damper on the theft of pharmaceuticals, while criminal syndicates saw a chance to become entrepreneurial. The black market expanded, flooding it with a bizarre assortment of substances of questionable origin. Smuggled heroin and cocaine often underwent dubious transformations. Psychedelic drugs like LSD had their origins in clandestine labs, where enterprising chemistry students ran operations in their back rooms or kitchens.

The Years of Living Dangerously

From the mid-60s to the mid-70s, UK culture underwent a seismic transformation. My comrades and I often travelled up to London, less than an hour away by train, where we ventured into the "underground" scene. Places like Middle Earth club in Covent Garden and the UFO club, part of the Roundhouse's events in Camden, beckoned with their promises of new experiences. Sometimes, we went to the East End or Brixton to buy various sorts of drugs.

One evening, a TV news item showed a conference at the Roundhouse where an assembly of intellectuals and activists from the US were giving credence to the subculture that we felt a part of. The media extolled their presence, and one of the speakers was holding up some flowers and talking about identifying with the 'flower power' movement of the hippies. My heart stirred with encouragement, for I believed myself to be walking the right path, an apostle of change.

In the early 1970s, I cast aside the trappings of conventional society, leaving a perfectly good job to go and live on government benefits in a commune. The large house in town became a centre for drug-taking and dealing. I immersed myself in this culture while rekindling the artistic spark I had left behind at college. My paintings found their way into the bohemian corners of our town. I designed and painted shop signs for clients in some of these offbeat places too.

As a close-knit group at the commune, we didn't regard our drug dealing as criminal activity. We were simply doing favours for our friends. Come what may we would be travelling to London to buy drugs for ourselves but if a wider group of individuals, not part of the commune, pressed us to get some for them, we were happy to provide. It was all fun and we could make money from it while engendering coolness in the eyes of our customers.

Yet, for all the leisurely indulgences, a darker underbelly was revealing itself. My emotions became a strange mix – often peace-loving, placid, timid, and fraught with self-doubt. But sometimes, fuelled by alcohol, I found myself entangled in brawls, each skirmish a losing battle. One fateful night a dear friend became a victim of a stabbing I had not witnessed. He told how he staggered down Southend High Street, bloodstained and desperate, calling out to passers-by for aid. Yet, in the eyes of those bystanders, he was just a 'druggie,' someone they dared not touch. Eventually, he found his way to hospital and recovered, but the emotional scars haunted him for years.

On another occasion, I got into a fight with someone at a party held on the upper floor of an apartment block. My foe and four or five of his friends seized me, dragged me to the outdoor landing, and threw me over the railing onto the concrete driveway below. I was lying unconscious in a pool of blood for a long time. An ambulance was called, and the police followed. My attackers fled, thinking they had killed me and would be arrested for murder. But against the odds, I survived. My face was smashed up, I had a broken jaw and ribs and some other wounds all of which eventually healed.

A young man I knew had dropped out at the same time as me and joined in the local drug scene. In less than two years he was having psychotic episodes. After one continuous bout of drug-taking over several days and nights, he had a breakdown, was taken away and admitted to a mental hospital.

Around the same time two of my favourite singers and musicians, Peter Green, founder of the band Fleetwood Mac and Syd Barratt of Pink Floyd, went through the same experiences. Drug-induced schizophrenia was the main problem, brought on by using LSD. These unsettling episodes, coupled with the bewildering behaviour of my friends, was becoming frightening. Anxiety clung to me and doubts about my own mental health scared me.

Amidst the chaos, the tide of sexual promiscuity swelled, gradually becoming the norm. I, too, was a participant, though there were boundaries I hesitated to cross. Perhaps it was the vestiges of my Catholic upbringing, or maybe it was simply a sense of prudishness that held me back from partaking in group sex during the haze of an LSD 'trip.' Friends urged me to "loosen up and embrace the changes," but for me, it was a bridge too far.

"Sexual freedom" was the guiding mantra, and rock music served as its Pied Piper. Songs boldly proclaimed the acceptability of pursuing carnal desires with whomever fate had thrown into one's path, even if you had just left a relationship. The concept of having three (or more) people in a relationship was introduced to us through various literary works and echoed in anthems like *Triad*, sung by Jefferson Airplane. The intoxicating rhythm of rock and the provocative words of literature were a potent influence that captivated us all and promised liberation.

The Uses of Literacy

Change had been sweeping through the world of the arts for decades, but by the 1950s, it had entered mainstream culture. In the 1960s authors become popular by writing books considered avant-garde or daring; D. H. Lawrence and Hemingway to name a couple. Some, like James Joyce, who had been conventional, I thought, began to write about things previously regarded as unmentionable. Some writers were instigators, while others hitched a ride on the wave of novelty, not wanting to be labelled "old-fashioned".

I was searching for something and read all the trendy books that were supposed to enlighten us: Hesse's *Steppenwolf* and *Siddhartha*, Huxley's *Brave New World* and *The Doors of Perception*, Orwell's *1984* and *Animal Farm* and Kahlil Gibran's *The Prophet*, and many others. These books, while interesting, offered no answers because everyone was starting to craft their own unique truth. You could mix and match various ideologies and spiritualities. Eastern religions were in vogue, though few truly grasped their essence, often merging them with paganism and the occult to forge peculiar creeds.

In these times, experimentation was the cool thing, whether it be with drugs, the occult, or speculative philosophies. There was even talk of a coming "Age of Aquarius" made popular by a chart-topping song. Linked to astrology, it heralded an era of peace, love, harmony, and enlightenment, a harbinger of the New Age. Some among us embraced this vision while others, considering the global turmoil, regarded it with scepticism.

I and my friends read *Supernature* as it was hailed a bestseller across the social spectrum. It sought to introduce the supernatural and occult to a wider audience, concepts once considered the province of the foolish. I championed this shift, believing in the importance of embracing the esoteric and making it an integral part of our daily lives. The author was making things like spiritual healing fashionable and suggesting that the supernatural should become a part of our everyday lives.

Let us not underestimate the profound influence wielded by pop and rock music. The Beatles, as they became increasingly famous, cast a mighty spell over the Western world, channelling the wisdom of American psychedelic guru Timothy Leary and the writings of Aldous Huxley to promote drug use and introduce Eastern religions to the masses. In the 1970s, David Bowie propelled us even further into the realm of the unconventional. As Ziggy Stardust, he wove a tapestry of transgenderism, extraterrestrial beings, defiance of societal norms, and rebellion through his songs and persona.

I, alongside fellow seekers, met in a local pub to dissect the transformation to a freer world. Initiating others into the world of drug use, getting them "turned on," played a pivotal role in this.

We congregated around a young man called Mark who was able to articulate what was going on in Western society. As a recent graduate, he was full of the ideas he had absorbed at university. In our debates we would listen to him talking about the books he was reading, often brought to the pub, which he recommended that we read – books about anti-consumerism, sexual repression, and sexual freedom.

I listened with rapt attention to these discussions but didn't say too much. I was afraid that a failure to clearly articulate any of my ideas would betray my ignorance, which was just beginning to attract my own notice.

Many films were being released into the mainstream that bore witness to the subversion of the status quo. Increasingly they included an anti-Christian theme. Christianity was portrayed as something holding back progress.

One movie expressed this fluently. *The Graduate*, starring Dustin Hoffman, told the story of a young man who had just finished university and wondering what he should do with his life. He gets into a forbidden relationship with a young woman promised to someone else. He gate-crashes her (arranged) wedding and the pair run off. Although essentially a love story, it employed evocative counterculture, rebellious and anti-Christian themes, and symbolism in the narrative. It attacked the perceived hypocrisy of Christian Middle America.

The mid 1960s to 70s also witnessed the greatest subversion of the newspaper and magazine industries. 1967 saw one edition of the *International Times* (*IT*) newspaper use its front page to show a picture of two naked men lying on a bed together. This was in support of a recently passed Parliamentary Bill that legalised homosexual sex between consenting adults. My friends were hardly surprised to learn that the Bill was supported by leaders of UK Churches including the then Archbishop of Canterbury. *IT*, along with other publications such as *Oz Magazine* and *Private Eye*, advocated free love, drug use and anti-establishment viewpoints. Many of these publications, which were very influential and had a wide circulation, became known as the underground press. In the commune there would be copies of a magazine called *High Times* lying around. One edition had, as its main feature, an article that discussed which was the best small light aircraft to buy or hire to smuggle drugs into the country.

It was an era where literature and media became tools for persuasion, an arena I had glimpsed during my time in Art School when the concept of Mass Media was heralded as an agent of change. All these elements converged, mounting an unrelenting assault on a society ill-prepared for the deluge of new philosophies. I revelled in the heady days of change.

Jack Kerouac's book *On the Road* permeated the zeitgeist, leading countless young souls on individualistic searches of self-discovery. Groups of friends embarked on journeys to remote corners of the country, establishing communes and striving to eke out a living from the land, despite their lack of agricultural know-how. It was a time of "doing your own thing," a creed that demanded non-interference.

In the US, this irrational behaviour became a crisis as thousands of parents filed missing persons reports for their children who had run away to San Francisco or the Woodstock Festival, answering the call of the counterculture.

I listened to the stories of friends and acquaintances returning from the "hippie trail," journeying through Morocco, residing on an Israeli kibbutz, trekking across the Middle East, and venturing onward to India and the Far East. Yet, they returned with no epiphanies to share. For many years I too had been searching for something, although I had not realised that I was on this quest, or what it was I was looking for.

My brother, Mick, the closest in age to me, had also veered off the beaten path. He had been in prison several times and, from the confines of prison, wrote me letters announcing a newfound Christianity. I suspected his conversion was a bid to curry favour with the prison authorities and secure an early release. When he eventually visited our commune house upon his release, I hesitated to introduce him to my cool, open-minded friends, fearing the stigma of having a "religious" brother.

Notes:

[1] Lysergic Acid Diethylamide, a powerful, synthetic, hallucinogenic drug.

[2] *San Francisco (Be Sure to Wear Flowers in your Hair)*, 1967, written by John Phillips and sung by Scott McKenzie, released on Ode Records in the US and Columbia Records in the UK.

Chapter 2

IN THE VALLEY OF DECISION

Things Fall Apart

As I have written, the mid-60s, with my grandmother's death, my mother's passing and "The Big Freeze," marked a time of coldness in my life – in more ways than one.

But if the extreme cold had its effect in 1963 then the extreme heat of 1976 had its impact on me in an even more profound way. 1976 was hot. Very hot!

It was dry throughout all the spring and summer months but June to August brought the worst drought in England since the 1720s. The drought was at its most severe in the Southwest of England. There were water shortages in many parts of the country and standpipes had to be erected in the streets where households could fill containers because water was no longer pumped into houses. It was not only the intense heat that affected us but also the length of time it went on for. Some places went without rain for 45 consecutive days. June and July temperatures were, in some places, around or well over 90°F (32.2°C). On the 3rd of July a temperature of 96.6°F (35.9°C) was recorded in Cheltenham.

On the 29th of July – said to be caused by the dry weather – a fire destroyed the pierhead at Southend Pier. The locals, including me, were proud of the Pier in a stupidly sentimental way. "The Longest Pier in the World" it said over the entrance. Suddenly there was talk of it being demolished.

That year brought further personal sadness. One of my sisters was dying of cancer and, having no money, I hitch-hiked up to Kings Lynn, where she was living, to say good-bye. She died shortly after. This pushed me even further into questioning the meaning of life and its purpose.

The commune had started with high ideals. We all agreed that members had to be working and paying their share of the rent. No drug dealing from the house. As time went on the stipulation to be working was downgraded to just an assurance that rent must be paid (wherever the money came from). Dealing became a problem and cannabis plants started to appear in various places in the house. People came and stayed, albeit for short periods of time, whose residency did not have the full support of all the members.

The police raided the premises on two separate occasions. This was at a time when police raids were virtually unheard of. The raids resulted in fines for some of us and gossipy copy for the local newspapers. Discussions about us shutting down the commune followed.

My brother Mick had been calling at the house or at local pubs, where he thought I'd be, trying to tell me about how he had become a Christian. I didn't believe him and argued strongly against the things he said. But I had a problem. I could not deny that he had changed. He was no longer the shifty person he had been. No longer appearing deceitful or evasive – as I still was then – he had a new persona that intrigued me.

I continued to argue with him over several months, but my resistance was waning.

That summer not only did God turn the heat up on the entire country, but he also turned the heat up on me; I was experiencing my own personal drought. I was doing all the things I had wanted to do but was left with an underlying tension.

There were various campaign groups those on the fringes of society could get involved with. I joined in seeing it as a way of helping others. 'Release' was an organisation that campaigned on behalf of those in prison for drug and drug-related offences. There were several groups whose goal was to see the legalisation of cannabis. A coalition of these organisations took over an empty shop near the town centre to promote 'community action'. This included changing drug laws, gay liberation, anti-war protests, environmental issues, and anti-consumerism.

I supported all the causes to some degree or another although I never expressed some deeper motivations that I had. I wanted to see a society that was broken down and dysfunctional. Such a society was desirable to me because there would be no laws restricting me and my friends from doing whatever we wanted.

During these years, my life, once fun-filled with friends, drugs, girls, and music, began to unravel. I had my art too, producing drawings and paintings mostly inspired by the lyrics of rock songs. I was doing all the things that should have satisfied me but always feeling there was something I lacked. I said to myself one day, I feel so dry – but it wasn't the weather.

I decided to investigate the 'Christian thing' Mick was bugging me about. If there was something in it or not, I'd find out. I needed to eliminate this irritating challenge so that I could get on with real searching.

I started asking deeper questions of Mick instead of simply being argumentative. I went with him to visit one of his Christian friends and then to a rehab centre for ex-offenders where he worked. He invited me there one evening because he was going to tell all the ex-cons the story of his conversion. I went hoping to expose trickery. After hearing his testimony, I felt challenged.

I had read out prayers and heard lots of prayers by others in the Catholic Church over the years, but they were meaningless rituals. That night I really prayed to God for the first time. It was a simple prayer: 'God, if you are there and you really have shown yourself to Mick, then could you please show yourself to me too?'

I also read a Christian book given to me by one of Mick's friends.

All this coincided with me leaving the commune. I had been living on my own in a small bedsit for a few weeks when God answered my weak prayer.

I was out of work and living off state benefits, so my change of address meant I had to re-apply for these hand-outs. Scraping together enough to fund a deposit at my new accommodation had left me without money but as the weeks went by the situation worsened. I had the worry of waiting for the Social Security Office to process my claim for rent money that my new landlord was chasing me for. For a long while I had not been able to buy drugs and, although this vexed me, it was, at the same time, causing me to think more clearly about my future. I had dropped out and lived the life I thought would satisfy me, but it had not lived up to its promise. I began to question the direction of my life as I was no longer enjoying it – or the weather. I usually loved hot summers, but the constant heat was getting to me.

Face to Face
Another hot day and I was walking the mile back to my bedsit from the town centre. With each step I felt increasingly burdened. A fearfulness was coming upon me. I couldn't understand its source.

It was early afternoon. The house was empty. I went upstairs and into my room. As soon as I shut the door, I felt as though there was someone else there. I looked around but there was no one. I went toward my bed.

No one was visible but I felt I was standing in front of someone. A person with supreme authority. I knew this person had the measure of me and that there was no trying to hoodwink him or put on a false front. But, more importantly for me, I could not, while he had me there, pretend anything to myself either. While I struggled to understand this encounter and its meaning, this person had no problems. He knew exactly what I was thinking and was in control of everything going on in that room.

Part of me was afraid but the sensation coming from this being informed me that, although he had total power and control of everything and it was right to fear him, I needn't be afraid. There was an assurance I would not be harmed. The terror I felt was suspended and a sense of overwhelming love penetrated every part.

I began to realise that this person was Jesus.

It might have been several hours, or it might have been half an hour. I lost all sense of time. I fell on the floor in front of him, crying at times, as he showed me my life. I was completely transfixed by visions or series of visions given to me.

I had a revelation of my selfishness. The last few years of my life had been particularly and deliberately selfish. I had left a perfectly good job and a responsible life to 'dropout', sponge off the state, live a hedonistic lifestyle, and take advantage of anyone I wished, particularly the women I met. Then it went deeper as I saw it was not just these last few years that was under scrutiny. The whole of my life had been selfish and self-centred. I had not acknowledged him in any way. I saw how wretched I was and that there was nothing good in me.

My sinful life had angered him, but, predominantly, it had saddened him. He had tried to reach out to me many times, but I had ignored him.

Then, I came face to face with the cross.

I was familiar with the story of Christ's crucifixion from my Catholic upbringing, but this experience was unlike any other. I had a vision of Jesus on the cross. At least, I think it was a vision. It wasn't like watching a video on a large screen. But I did see something—something more vividly and forcefully than any technological device could transmit.

Seemingly transported back in time, I witnessed Jesus on the cross. My head was at the same level as His, so I must have been hovering in the air somehow. Mere metres away, I saw the pain, agony, and distress on His face. His body was covered in blood. I could smell it along with the stench of sweat and other odours.

I was aware of being on a busy public highway, with lots of noise and voices shouting. Although I could not see the lower part of His body, I knew He was naked. Awareness of these surrounding details faded as I focused on His face. I didn't want to look at Him. I wanted to look away.

Gazing into His eyes, our souls locked in communion.

I knew the traditional story: Jesus took the punishment for our sins. I had known this in an indistinct way, but now I was experiencing it. I grasped that He wasn't just dying for humanity collectively but for me personally.

The weight of this truth overwhelmed me. I was unworthy of such a sacrifice. An understanding came to me: the entirety of humanity, me included, teetered on the precipice of hell, burdened by collective sin, and I was responsible for my part in this. As I reflected on my life and acknowledged my ignorance of Him, a burning question surfaced, whether spoken audibly or in my heart I wasn't sure, but I was shouting at Him: "Why me? I'm not worthy of this. Why do You care?"

"Because I love you."

He was saying that despite all my sin and selfishness, he still loved me and wanted me. He was telling me to forget about everyone else for a minute and try to grasp that he loved me and wanted a relationship with me personally. He always had.

I was completely undone. I could not go anywhere or do another single thing in my entire life until I had responded to this.

Part of this unveiling included an all-important command to believe what was being revealed and then either obey by calling upon Him to save me from my sinful state or, continue as I was.

With the passage of time still blurred, I went through a process of firstly realising that I was on my way to hell if I stayed as I was, and then reordering my life to avoid that fate. I asked for forgiveness for all that I had done wrong. I promised to listen to him in the future. I didn't have a clue what it would mean in practice, but I vowed to follow him.

As the afternoon waned, I felt a lightness within, as if He had lifted me from the depths of despair and dusted me off. Hope permeated my soul, and despite doubts about living a consistently "good life," I clung to His assurance that, together, we would navigate the way forward.

Now I See

Over the following days I tried to tell friends about what had happened. I began to see and understand things that I had not learnt or been told.

I knew for sure that Jesus was God.

The true condition of everyone's lives was revealed to me. The curtain that hides the spiritual reality of all that happens on earth was pulled back. I saw the battle between good and evil. The whole world as it was then and everything that had gone on throughout all of history was and is, all about Jesus; his love for mankind and the wicked deceitfulness that the devil uses to blind people's eyes to this. All the good and the bad things that had happened in my own life and family I could now see clearly as part of this struggle. I knew that I had been on my way to hell but through my encounter with Jesus and getting right with God I had been saved from that.

With these newfound insights, I had peace and an assurance that everything would be all right. With little money or possessions, I could sit and eat a meagre meal in my bedsit room with gladness in my heart because I had come to know him and was sure I was saved.

Pondering the utopian ideals of the dropout culture and the hippie movement I had believed in; I could now see them as futile. They had promised a life – a world even – of peace and love if only we could all get on together.

The enchanting 1970 Joni Mitchell song about the US Woodstock Festival had vocalised it so beautifully. It elevated humanity and suggested that we could get back to a life as lived in the Garden of Eden. But, of course, we can't do that without God. He showed me they were delusions.

I had thought that socialism had the answers to mend a society that was falling apart. But once my eyes had been opened, I realised that these ideas were fantasies invented by human minds and would provide no solutions for society's ills. I marvelled at how I and others in society had been so stupid to have believed the devil's tricks.

I had enjoyed the meetings with groups of friends where we discussed and tried to understand deeper issues but had to admit to myself that we had never come to any rational conclusions. I recognised that my friends and I had been deceived by hidden influences. The devil's most cunning trick was convincing us that he didn't exist or that he was an abstract force. My friends were ensnared in various ways, unable to fathom the truth I now saw. As I tried to tell them what had happened to me many resisted and grew hostile, recoiling from the idea that they faced the consequences of their actions. Some argued from a position of what seemed good judgement and knowledge gained through what they had absorbed at university. They tried to convince me that my conversion experience was a delusion that I would soon recover from.

I began asking Jesus to reveal himself to them as he had with me. I created a list of people and began talking to God about them, but it got so long I had to break it down into seven daily sections. As time went by and with great sadness, I realised that I had to distance myself from my friends. They expected me to continue living as I had before, embracing their lifestyle, but I had been extracted from a world filled with deceit and lies. I was moving in the opposite direction, led by my newfound faith.

The Hand You Shake

One afternoon, as I prayed and thanked God for saving me, something extraordinary happened. His presence enveloped me in a unique way, and I felt a powerful sense of approval. It was as though God was confirming that I was His, and He would lead me. I had a powerful revelatory experience of Him as a father, watching over me, guiding me through life on Earth and into eternity. He assured me that I was now His adopted child. This experience might have been what some call the infilling of the Holy Spirit, sealing His salvation promises forever.

My brother Mick noticed my conversion and gifted me a Bible, a first for me. I delved into the Gospels, where I encountered the remarkable stories of Jesus and the incredible feats of early believers in the book of Acts. Through reading and conversation with the Author, I began to grasp the depth of my newfound faith. I had initially shaken hands with a stranger, but now, as I engaged with the Bible, our relationship deepened. I realised God was far bigger and more powerful than I had initially imagined. I came to appreciate the extraordinary gift of salvation. My part was merely to cry out to God in my weakness, and, in return, I received countless blessings, including the promise of eternal life.

Another gift I began to unpack was that of repentance. Before my salvation, I had not been inclined to repent for my sins, my lifestyle, or my rejection of God. I hadn't even realised I was in the wrong. However, when a holy God opens your eyes, your perspective changes. I discovered in the Bible how new believers, as a sign of setting their lives in order, would make amends wherever possible, especially if their wrongdoing had affected others.

Before I "dropped out," I worked at a DIY wholesale warehouse where I used to steal items and sell them to a local shopkeeper who had ordered them. I felt compelled to go back confess to my previous boss and offer to repay any money I owed, despite the possibility of prosecution due to my prior police record. Surprisingly, my boss forgave me. I made it clear that my transformation was the result of my newfound faith.

I also had a fine for a drug offence that I started to pay off but eventually stopped. I returned to the court offices to make arrangements to continue payment, which were readily accepted. Again, I could have got into trouble for dodging the fine but there was no further action.

Shortly after "dropping out," I had intentionally overdrawn my bank account with no intention of settling the debt. However, after becoming a believer, I went back and arranged to repay the debt.

After my conversion and returning to work, I confronted a significant debt. While living with a woman before my conversion, we had purchased a house together, and she had borrowed a substantial sum from her parents for the deposit and to cover financial difficulties. After our separation, I had failed to repay my share of the debt. God challenged me over this. I hired a solicitor to negotiate the payments, and, over a few years, I settled the debt.

I also felt compelled to apologise to people, including family members, for my past behaviour and mistreatment. The Bible emphasised that I should both repent and believe, and not just in words but through actions.

One day, I returned to my bedsit after a walk in the town. As was my usual habit, I attempted to roll a cigarette, when I suddenly felt the presence of God as if He were in the room, watching me from a chair. I couldn't continue; I was ashamed and fearful. I couldn't roll a cigarette in the presence of God. I closed the tobacco tin and never opened it again.

I had a history of getting involved with different women whenever the opportunity arose, sometimes even living with them. However, I realised that I could no longer continue this practice. I understood that sex outside of marriage went against God's guidelines for our well-being. I had to wait for God to lead me in the right direction regarding relationships.

The Narrow Path.

A few weeks after my conversion, my brother introduced me to a Christian couple who lived a few miles outside Southend. We clicked instantly, and, to cut a long story short, I ended up living with them and their family for three years, though it was initially intended as a short-term rehabilitation period. My goal was to find a job and cultivate a disciplined lifestyle.

Their unselfishness in opening their home to me provided the perfect environment to establish my faith and resist the temptation to return to my old lifestyle. It was an incredible display of God's kindness and grace.

Upon joining the family, I faced a crucial choice: to live in a separate "granny flat" they had in the extension or to live with the family. While my natural inclination was to live on my own,

I recognised that it might give me room for sinful behaviour. I could have lived a partially Christian life but slipped into my old habits when alone. The enemy tempted me, but God challenged me. I knew the stakes and decided to follow Jesus wholeheartedly, living transparently in front of the Christian family. I'm grateful I made the right choice.

The family I lived with were members of a local Anglican church, and during this time, I began to understand the concept of "church." I started attending services regularly, initially feeling awkward but eventually becoming enthusiastic about it. It was inspiring to meet others who, like me, had encountered God. I felt a close and pleasant bond with fellow believers. We were brothers and sisters who shared a common faith. I began to understand what church is.

However, I was puzzled that some churchgoers didn't appear to be born again. I tried to share my experience of finding Jesus with them, but they showed little interest and advised me against discussing my conversion experience, fearing it might discourage potential seekers. Confused, I sought guidance from God. This was when God revealed to me the true meaning of church and how not everything that appears to be 'church' truly embodies it.

Now might be a good time to consider what the word 'church' really means. The clearest description I have found comes from a book by Ron Trudinger in which he shows that the Greek New Testament has only one word translated church. Despite the confusing secondary meanings given to it over the centuries, its original meaning is clear and simple and clearly related to our word call.[1]

Trudinger, by using some technical word building, extracts the meaning from its Latin and Greek roots and shows how the original word, Ecclesia, means "called out ones". He points out several clear deductions from this. Ecclesia refers to people; it's a collective term meaning a group of people and he goes on to make clear that church is not a building or a community centre and not a preaching centre.

I looked forward to joining with other people to whom that same miraculous thing had happened. Meeting together with other believers at different times and places, usually not in a church building, strengthened my faith.

The Story So Far

I hope to have given you a glimpse into my early life, the factors that led to my conversion, and the subsequent spiritual growth. I aim not to sensationalise or shock readers needlessly. While I could include some lurid details I'm now ashamed of, my goal is to show that I was just as lost as other wayward young people were then. I want to connect with them and anyone else who is far from God or caught up in a destructive lifestyle. I also want to show how we are all vulnerable to being led astray by influences outside of ourselves.

I write with a purpose, and that purpose will become evident later. I've shared my background and the world that I was immersed in and how I was called out of that.

Notes:
[1] Trudinger, R. (1979), *Cells for Life*, Plainfield, New Jersey, Logos International, p12-13.

Chapter 3

WHERE I SAT AND WHERE I WENT

The View from Here

This section doesn't concern the pew I occupied while attending an Anglican church in late 1970s Essex (the pews were replaced with comfortable chairs soon after anyway). It's about the position I took on matters related to my faith and the church. My viewpoint was formed over many years, shaped by a strong desire to witness the growth of the 'true church' locally and nationally, influenced by the churches I attended and the leaders I encountered. It began to be established in the late 1970s when I became a believer and continued evolving until 2017 when, due to God's intervention, my perspective changed.

Walking with God

Early on, I grappled with the issue of water baptism. Having been raised a Roman Catholic and christened as a baby, my newfound faith was a stark departure from my Catholic upbringing. I was eager to obey Jesus's command in Scripture: repent and be baptised. The Bible clearly states that baptism is for believers, so I approached the Rector to inquire about adult baptism by full immersion. Unfortunately, he couldn't accommodate my request due to the constraints of the Anglican Church.

The family I was staying with directed me to an independent evangelical church with a minister willing to baptise me upon a public confession of faith. I invited family and some friends to the event, but regrettably, none attended.

The Anglican church I later joined was grappling with what was then termed the Renewal Movement. During this period, God was revealing the importance of receiving the power of the

Holy Spirit to some church leaders and members. This led to varying responses, with some churches embracing the gifts of the Spirit and more freedom in worship, while others staunchly opposed it. Some believed that the gifts of the Spirit had ceased with the Apostles and considered speaking in tongues as 'of the devil.' This disagreement caused church splits, prompting many to join congregations where Renewal wasn't occurring.

The Rector attempted to bridge the divide by retaining traditional Anglican services but adding Sunday evening and midweek praise and worship gatherings where the gifts of the Spirit were allowed. I attended some of these house group-style meetings at the Rectory, where the presence of God was palpable. On at least two occasions, prominent church members openly wept as God convicted them of sin, leading them to confess and seek prayer for repentance. God's love filled the room as they received forgiveness through the prayers of others, leaving a profound impact on me and reinforcing the gravity of our faith journey.

Some, like me, regarded this move of the Spirit as a revival for the church. I believed that allowing God's power to flow would make the church more effective in our communities and rekindle our sense of purpose: to be a beacon in society and share the Gospel. Others in the church shared this enthusiasm.

I was intensely committed to my faith, and in retrospect, I may have been a bit too fervent. However, I believe that there's no such thing as being too passionate about following Jesus.

Sharing the Gospel – Sometimes Using Words

After my conversion, I returned to the printing company where I had worked before 'dropping out'. During my lunch breaks, I would read a small New Testament daily, often rereading it immediately upon finishing.

Before my conversion, I struggled to maintain employment, frequently moving from one job to another due to lateness and absences caused by a form of depression. Upon my return, one of the owners who had known me previously was astounded by the change in my work habits. I was now punctual and consistent.

From the start, I resolved to be bold and honest about my newfound faith, not necessarily through words but because of how I lived. One day, the manager asked me about my beliefs, saying, "What is this religion you follow?"

I devoted significant time talking to God about family members and friends. The couple who had taken me in shared the story of a local woman, a fellow believer, who was struggling with her faith. I prayed for her, and during a moment of prayer, God spoke clearly about His love for her. I wrote down His compassionate words and, not knowing what should be done with such information, shared them with my hosts. The note was taken to the woman who, upon reading it, burst into tears and asked for prayer, finding renewed encouragement in her walk with the Lord.

My prayer life inevitably led to a desire for evangelism, an earnest longing to share the message of Jesus. While prayer made me aware of God's love for non-believers, it also compelled me to grasp the seriousness of His warnings for those who deliberately turned away from Him, as I once had. Fuelled by concern for their souls, I confronted a mocking co-worker, exclaiming with a mix of concern and what I later learned was called righteous anger, "Don't you fear God?!"

On Mission

I spent my first bit of annual leave after returning to work joining an outreach mission in Watford for two weeks. It was a tent mission organised by Good News Crusade (GNC) and supported by local churches in Watford. Engaging in evangelism was exhilarating. I found leading someone to Christ one of the most fulfilling things anyone could ever do. The following year, I made a bold decision. I planned to dedicate my entire summer, four months, working with GNC, as part of their 'Temporary Team', which meant leaving my job at the printing company. I prayed about it and felt strongly led to go, trusting that God would provide.

During that year, GNC embarked on its most extended mission, running three Christian Family Camps and three missions in towns across the UK, as far apart as Leamington Spa and the Lake District. My savings quickly depleted. The temporary staff received no wages, but collections were taken at the end of each event. Living by faith was the way, while I remained committed to paying off my debts back home.

The Lord provided abundantly during my time away, even granting something I hadn't dared to ask for. I'd never been to the Lake District, and I longed to capture its beauty with my own camera. Though I initially hesitated to request such a personal desire, a gift from my home church included enough extra cash for that camera. The kindness of God overwhelmed me, melting my heart.

At the summer's end, I stopped by the printing works, hoping for some part-time work. My post had been filled following my absence, but the person who replaced me had just resigned. I was offered my old job back, a clear testament to God's care.

On another occasion at the printing works a rather sombre but puzzling set of events unfolded. The foreman shared the difficulties of the cleaning lady, who often took time off to care for her supposedly ill husband. Passing by her one day, I had a profound experience. The Lord revealed to me that her husband wasn't ill; she was poisoning him. I was shocked and, having never experienced such a thing before, unsure of what to do, I continued my tasks, intending to seek God's guidance later. As I left work and prayed, the unsettling revelation lingered in my mind. I asked God for confirmation. What was I meant to do with this information? Because it was a disturbing experience I asked for another sign or for someone else to receive the same message.

Maybe the cleaning lady stopped working there, as I later forgot about the issue.

Several years later, having left that employment and moved away, I made a return visit to Essex, and called in on my former colleagues. In our conversation, we talked about the cleaning lady, and I discovered that she had indeed been poisoning her husband, ultimately leading to his death. She consistently used small amounts of weed killer over a long period of time so that it appeared as if he was ill. Due to complications during the investigation, she escaped arrest but was later found out and sentenced to life imprisonment. "The Paraquat Poisoner" became a well-known murder case in that part of the county.

I still don't understand why God revealed her wrongdoing to me. I agonised over whether I should have confronted her or sought advice from a spiritually mature Christian. But the prayers I made at the time covered every eventuality and were an act of handing everything over to God. Why, as time went on, he allowed the crime to be committed I do not know. I have tried to figure it out many times but have had to conclude that I must leave it with him.

Back in our church, our passion for sharing the Gospel motivated us to launch a local outreach program named Evangelism Explosion. This method provided an effective way to communicate truth to unbelievers. The Anglican Church had an advantage with locals inquiring about marriage and christenings, creating opportunities for gospel sharing.

Our evangelism programme was going well, and then we heard of some new teaching that promised to give it – and all our church activities – more impetus.

A Fork in the Road

In the late 1970s and early '80s, some church members began attending the Dales Bible Weeks in Harrogate, Yorkshire. We discovered new insights about the church's potential as a significant force both nationally and globally. These revelations unveiled a more exciting path than the old, traditional ways, as the church in the UK was being perceived as largely irrelevant and outdated.

The message of the Bible Weeks brought anticipation and excitement to Christians who were frustrated by how the world perceived the church. The speakers at these events explained how a great revival was on the horizon, driven by the promises in the scriptures. Prophecies from the Old Testament, which were being applied to the church, filled us with hope. Some of the new teaching featured in a song we all sang enthusiastically. It was inspired by some verses from the book of Isaiah:

Arise, shine, for your light has come,
and the glory of the LORD rises upon you.
For behold, darkness covers the earth,
and thick darkness is over the peoples;
but the LORD will rise upon you,
and His glory will appear over you.
Nations will come to your light,
and kings to the brightness of your dawn.
Isaiah 60: 1-3.

The teachers of this new way explained that while the world would become spiritually darker, this would be inconsequential because the church would shine more brightly and overcome the darkness. It was taught that many people will come to this light and become Christians – whole nations!

The first part of Isaiah chapter 2 revealed similar promises from the Lord:

In the last days the mountain of the
house of the Lord's temple
will be established as the chief of the mountains;
it will be exalted above the hills,
and all nations will stream to it.
And many peoples will come and say:
"Come, let us go up to the mountain of the LORD,
to the temple of the God of Jacob.
He will teach us His ways
so that we may walk in His paths. "
The law will go out from Zion,
the word of the Lord from Jerusalem.
He will judge between many the nations
and will settle disputes for many peoples.
They will beat their swords into plowshares

and their spears into pruning hooks.
Nation will not take up sword against nation,
nor will they train for war anymore.
Isaiah 2: 2-4.

This prophecy is repeated in Micah 4: 1-4.

Although these verses were originally addressed to the nation of Israel, we were taught that they now applied to the church, as it had become the New Israel. The Jews had rejected Jesus as their Messiah and were subsequently rejected by God. The physical land of Israel was no longer significant, and any references to territory should be seen as 'spiritual territory' that we, the church, could occupy by infiltrating various aspects of society. In a similar vein, another new hymn we all sang took verses from the Bible to say that the church is here for the healing of the nations. This realisation was empowering for the churches and ignited a passion for evangelism.

It was equally exciting to be encouraged to claim power as individual Christians. Bible teachers informed us that we could operate in the same way as Jesus by asserting dominion over challenging situations and the natural world. Jesus had come to restore dominion to humanity, a dominion we had lost. We were now to claim it by performing miracles, healings, and deliverance, thereby establishing the Kingdom or Government of God on Earth.

This task was being aided by the restoration of the offices of the Ephesians 4:11 ministries, particularly those of the Apostle and Prophet. It was a heady concept. Verses from Isaiah were cited to describe the actions of the church as it reclaimed the world for God:

Your people will rebuild the ancient ruins;
you will restore the age-old foundations;
you will be called Repairer of the Breach,
Restorer of the Streets of Dwelling.
Isaiah 58: 12

Reports surfaced of Christians moving into the deprived areas of UK towns, renovating houses, and revitalising the localities, validating this new idea.

The teachings were enriched by prophecies. One prophecy, shared at a Bible Week, painted a mesmerising picture of a pure white flower sprouting from a pile of straw and dung left behind by animals. This symbolised the church's growth in visibility and purity and was conveyed through a dreamlike song, captivating the listeners.

We were in awe of the speakers who graced the Dales Bible Weeks and other venues. They exuded confidence, authority, and persuasiveness in delivering their messages. The Dales teachings evolved into what was termed "Restorationism," a concept drawn from Acts 3:21, signifying God's intention to restore everything in the world through the Church.

However, the movement did have its pitfalls. The leadership divided into several groups in the North of England, Wales, and the South. The two major groups were known as R1 and R2. Another problem within Restorationism was "Heavy Shepherding," which demanded strict obedience to church leaders, even in personal life decisions for individual members. Disobeying the elders' directives was often perceived as rebellion.

Despite these difficulties, it became popular for groups of Christians from established churches to leave and form small gatherings in people's homes, known as the House Church Movement. Restorationism became established in the '80s and '90s, even having its own magazine.

Nevertheless, the revered leaders in the Restoration churches, despite their compelling speeches, revealed some dangers as the movement splintered. These leaders, guiding large groups of believers along this new path, were not infallible.

While I remained loyal to my local Anglican church, I grew disheartened by the system it represented. At the local level, there were battles over accepting the work of the Holy Spirit, while at the national level, there was a gradual abandonment of belief in the authority of scripture. Many clergy denied fundamental Christian doctrines. David Jenkins, consecrated as the Bishop of Durham in July 1984, publicly professed disbelief in the Virgin Birth and the physical resurrection of Jesus. Lightning struck York Minster three days after his consecration, causing considerable damage but no injuries.

Some in our local church saw this as a sign from God, while Church of England officials dismissed it as a coincidence, revealing a belief that God no longer intervened in such ways. Jenkins went on to bless a gay civil partnership and was banned from several churches due to his erroneous beliefs and occasional use of profanity while preaching.

The growing rejection of biblical truth prompted our rector and a team of leaders to establish an organisation called Action for Biblical Witness in Our Nation (ABWON) with the goal of countering the drift into apostasy. The rector was elected to the Church of England Synod but found himself under overwhelming pressure to conform to the organisation's traditional 'broad church' approach, emphasising 'unity with diversity.'

Despite my deep affection for the members of my local congregation, I welcomed an opportunity offered me to work with the organisation I had been on a mission with. GNC was based in Cornwall, allowing me to become part of an independent free church and further pursue my passion for mission.

Personal Journeys

In 1980, I married a wonderful young woman I had met in the local church in Essex. It was satisfying to know I had found someone I wanted to spend the rest of my life with. It was a big part of the desperate search I had been immersed in before my conversion. I'm sure that all my friends from that time were looking for the same contentment but, because they gave in to the erratic influences of the day, they never found it.

In 1983, we welcomed our first child, and shortly after, I was settling into my new job in Cornwall. This marked the beginning of a lifelong career in publicity and media production, predominantly within Christian contexts.

We settled in Cornwall, actively engaging in the local church. I worked with itinerant evangelist Don Double, who orchestrated tent missions, teaching conferences, and some of the UK's earliest Christian camps. Our collaboration operated on exciting faith-based principles; there was no salary guarantee. While we did receive payment, it was never assured, as the ministry relied on donations and gifts. We had to embrace a lifestyle of faith, uncertain about regular income. Our "home church" in Essex supported us to some degree because they viewed our venture as us being sent out to do missionary work. Numerous instances stand as testimony to God's grace, including surprise monetary gifts and bags of food left on our doorstep.

Our years in Cornwall, with our growing family, were consistently driven by a passion for mission. In addition to my media work in the headquarters of GNC, I continued participating in various missions.

A big part of Don Double's evangelistic messages included prayer for healing. I sometimes found myself facing a queue of sick people requesting prayer following an appeal by Don in a tent mission or Christian camp meeting. My wife and I sometimes ministered together in this way.

Our dedication to outreach also influenced our personal lives. We frequently interacted with a diverse array of individuals who were struggling, whether with mental health challenges, homelessness, or addiction. Our home often became a place for them to share a meal with us. My oldest daughter fondly remembers her childhood with light-hearted humour, saying, "What I remember about growing up is that our house was always full of weirdos." This was not meant disrespectfully; it was a reminder that, before my conversion, I too needed love and grace to transform my life.

I want readers to understand that my Christian life was not always without anxiety or challenges. My childhood distress often left me struggling to cope with daily life. Even simple tasks like getting up and going to work were overwhelmed me at times.

After becoming a believer, I experienced an initial period of euphoria for a year or two. However, old fears and self-doubt eventually resurfaced. Sometimes, I would disappear for hours, sometimes even a day or two, wandering aimlessly in a depressive haze. I am grateful for my patient wife, who endured my troubling behaviour with resilience.

Shortly after moving to Cornwall, my struggles reached a tipping point, necessitating action, but God intervened. One Sunday, a Bible teacher visited our church and, without prior knowledge, spoke insightfully about past trauma related to my mother's alcoholism but particularly the condition of being fatherless. He offered special prayers for me, and I was delivered from the affliction that had troubled me for so long.

This experience partly explains my empathy for others who struggled with life.

The independent church we attended was overseen by a small group of elders. While it offered freedom from the constraints of traditional churches, it seemed somewhat unstable in its administration. Immorality among the leadership was exposed, there were frequent changes in the eldership, the fellowship's name, and meeting venues.

Then, around 1994, something uplifting happened.

As the 'free' churches and house churches that had formed from the old traditional systems began to lose their way, another appealing alternative route appeared which brought a renewed hope. This path had the potential to stir up the church again, fulfilling the desires of many Christians for a revival in their time.

THE TIDE HAS TURNED

Chapter 4

A BLESSING FOR THE CHURCH

Believe It and Receive It

Leaders from a church in Cornwall had returned from meetings in London, bringing back a "blessing" that could be passed on through the laying on of hands, just as they had received it.

This "blessing" had been sweeping through their church for weeks when a group from our church, including me, went to investigate. Like most churches in the UK, we had heard about the revival that had started in Toronto, Canada. There were reports of church members being overwhelmed by the Holy Spirit, often falling to the floor and bursting into fits of laughter. One evening, we decided to see it for ourselves.

The church we visited met in a school, and the assembly hall was packed with eager members from various churches, all curious about the 'Toronto Blessing.' The pastor spoke briefly and then prayed for some of his congregation to receive this blessing. Many volunteered, and some fell, crying out as if in pain, while others began laughing uncontrollably and rolling on the floor. We were told these manifestations were the Holy Spirit's work, often leading to emotional healing and empowering the church for 'power evangelism.'

It was akin to drunken behaviour, and we were reminded that the disciples on the day of Pentecost were similarly accused of drunkenness. They went on to evangelise powerfully and perform miracles (see Acts chapter 2). We were urged not to be afraid and to trust that God was doing something new beyond our understanding.

I prayed fervently, questioning whether this was God's work

or some deception. The idea of being filled with God's Spirit and liberated to do mighty things for Him appealed to me.

The meeting's leader offered to pray for anyone wanting to receive the blessing, and all our church representatives, including myself, raised our hands. I had reservations but didn't want to seem reluctant; I desperately wanted to believe this was true.

Over the following months and years, the Toronto Blessing and its manifestations became part of church life in many different places across the UK.

Embracing the 'New Church' Vision

After working with Don Double's organisation, I started a graphic design, print, and publishing business that ran for about seven years. However, financial problems forced me to close it down. Then, my brother Mick, now married with children, had relocated from London to Bedford. Coincidentally, my wife's parents and youngest sister had also moved there.

The lack of work in Cornwall compelled us to move to Bedford with our growing family, which now included three children. Our last year in Cornwall led us to join the Bible Week at Stoneleigh, Warwickshire. Mick attended a church belonging to the group running this event called New Frontiers. I was impressed with their organisation, led by Terry Virgo, who had been instrumental in the Dales Bible weeks and the Restorationist movement. He had also initiated the Downs Bible Weeks because of church plants along the South Coast.

Home groups began forming as numerous dissatisfied believers left traditional churches to join the emerging House Church Movement. Similar movements like Pioneer, Ichthus, Vineyard, and others cropped up, collectively known as New Churches. New Frontiers aimed to reshape Christianity in the UK, distancing itself from traditional denominations and advocating churches rooted in New Testament principles, free from bureaucratic church systems.

There was a growing idea that denominations had not been

God's plan, and rather than attempting to reform them from within, it was better to start anew. I wholeheartedly agreed with this perspective. I desired to be part of a church aligned with God's will, distinct from other denominations, what I considered the 'true Church.' It was thought that all historic churches would eventually join as they became enlightened.

In 1998, my family and I moved to Bedford, where I was thrilled to join a New Church. I enthusiastically engaged in various activities within the church, including working with children, participating in missions, leading home groups, and taking a prominent role in the emerging prophetic ministry.

We attended further Stoneleigh Bible Weeks, where we heard motivating messages about the church's growth. A particularly stirring vision was presented to us about 'Joel's Army,' based on an account in the book of Joel. We were encouraged to become this army and impact our local communities, ultimately leading to the church's worldwide dominion. Songs based on this idea were written and sung.

Other Old Testament passages, such as the valley of dry bones (Ezekiel 37:1-14), and Isaiah 54:2-3, urging the church to expand and strengthen, were frequently explained to congregations at camps, Leaders Conferences, and in the churches. We were often reminded of Revelation 5, which speaks of a diverse, global church.

Much of the New Churches' teaching was strongly influenced by John Wimber, a church leader from America, who emphasised Restorationism and Power Evangelism in the early 1990s.

Another captivating aspect of these new churches was their emphasis on grace. Numerous books, teachings and songs focussed on this concept. It was uplifting to be told that God was not an irate tyrant always watching to see if we made a mistake.

My Enthusiasm for 'New Church'

Upon our move to Bedford, I completed a degree in journalism and media that I had begun in Cornwall. For my final dissertation, I penned a series of feature articles for both secular and Christian presses, shedding light on the roots, burgeoning popularity, and growing influence of the New Churches within the UK ecclesiastical landscape. My articles brimmed with praise and enthusiasm for the new movement.

I drew material from various sources including books, magazine articles, papers authored by key proponents, and interviews with prominent figures. Notably, I vividly recall engaging in an hour-long telephone interview with Terry Virgo, then leader of New Frontiers, as well as meeting another member of the organisation in a restaurant at Waterloo Station.

While covering a spectrum of topics, the overarching objective of my articles remained singular: to prompt both the nation and established churches to contemplate the remarkable transformations unfolding within the religious milieu of the UK.

I articulated how, in a postcolonial, post-Christian Britain, missionaries from nations to which we originally disseminated the gospel were now returning to rekindle the flame of that same gospel, which they asserted we had forsaken. This piece was inspired by Indian evangelist Ram Babu who was visiting Bedford to conduct a series of meetings.

One extensive article delved into the historical trajectory of the New Churches, their burgeoning growth, and the Christian festivals and camps they spawned. Additionally, other articles scrutinised revivals in the UK and worldwide, as well as the media platforms propagating and reporting on them. Notably, I conducted an in-depth investigation into the genesis and evolution of what is now recognised as GOD TV.

Among the narratives shared was the poignant account of John Gillespie, a Methodist minister compelled to depart from his denomination due to his vocal dissent against its departure from scripture, its escalating liberalism, and its embrace of interfaith policies. Despite encountering initial challenges, and persecution from those who remained, Gillespie and his congregation persevered, eventually witnessing the flourishing of their new church. Furthermore, the piece highlighted the exodus of other ministers from their denominations to establish New Churches, underscoring the disparity between the rigid structures of traditional churches and the vitality, dynamism, and innovation inherent in the emergent ones.

Additionally, on behalf of the church, I wrote advertorials for the local secular newspaper, sharing stories of people healed at Ram Babu's meetings. Later, I worked in the editorial office of that newspaper, though this was a secular role. Nevertheless, my work for the church reflected my eagerness to promote it, its founding organisation, and its activities.

Many of these articles are available to read now. See *My Enthusiasm for 'New Church'* in the Appendix listings.

Expectation Grows

The manifestations of the Toronto Blessing continued at our local New Frontiers church in Bedford, as well as at Leaders Conferences in Brighton and other gatherings. Home group and church meetings were filled with stories of people witnessing gold dust and receiving gold fillings in their teeth. Some had visions and encounters with angels. I knew someone who was so moved by these manifestations that he sold his house and relocated to Toronto to be at the epicentre of the movement. Like him, I was eager to be wherever God was at work, attending various conferences and meetings where I believed the Spirit was active.

One manifestation stemming from the Blessing was the 'Toronto Twitch.' Believers who had received the Blessing would involuntarily jerk, shake, or twitch during homegroups and prayer meetings. These spasms were sometimes accompanied by vocal exclamations like shouts or shrieks. I also developed a muscular twitch that seemed to originate from my abdomen.

Leaders in our churches publicly displayed these phenomena, often jerking and twisting their bodies while preaching, sometimes with bouts of laughter. Prominent figures in the church endorsed and promoted these signs, creating a heightened sense of anticipation that something significant was about to happen.

Revival was a constant topic of discussion, and I was excited when it began to take shape in the US in 2008 in Lakeland, Florida. A previous revival had occurred in Brownsville, Pensacola, in 1995, causing a sensation for a while. The Lakeland revival was particularly thrilling because God was using an ordinary-looking man with numerous tattoos, Todd Bentley. I would stay up late into the night watching him on the TV's God Channel as the revival spread, even reaching other parts of the US and internationally. He would lay hands on people seeking healing, and they would fall, being 'slain in the spirit.'

Our local church convened a special meeting to address these developments, as there was much speculation and uncertainty. An elder reassured us, explaining that we should not fear these extraordinary events, as God can use various means and people to accomplish His purposes. I concurred with this assessment. God was undoubtedly on the move, and we needed to move with Him. I became enthusiastic about seeing signs, wonders, and healing. I intensified my practice of sharing words of knowledge and prophesying in church meetings. On one occasion, I gave a word of knowledge about a person with a leg injury, accurately describing the injury and when it had occurred. Someone responded, and I prayed for their healing.

One of my prophetic insights, a vision of a mother eagle shaking her nest to encourage her baby eagles to leave, was impactful in our church. I interpreted it as a sign that God wanted to shake up the church to make signs, wonders, and healing more frequent. I shared this during a church prayer meeting, and an elder encouraged me to act it out by physically shaking anyone who felt the need for spiritual awakening. While not many people initially responded, as I went around the room, another elder eventually requested prayer. A couple of months later, he left to pastor another church in a different part of the country. Unbeknown to most, he had been discontented for some time. In his farewell speech, he attributed his departure to the 'shaking event,' saying it had triggered a change in his spiritual life. I couldn't understand how my prophetic message had led him to leave; it was meant to encourage believers to be more open to the work of the Spirit, not to drive them away.

The phenomenon of 'Treasure Hunting' was gaining popularity, and I often joined groups of believers on the streets to locate and pray for people we believed God had directed us to, often for healing. I want to emphasise that then relatively few Christians were engaged in these activities in Bedford, or to my knowledge, in the entire country.

It was then that I led a church homegroup and encouraged complete openness to spiritual experiences in our meetings. I provided sections from a book called Megashift for group members to read. This book featured reports from individuals around the world who had encountered strange signs, wonders, and miracles. I aimed to inspire the group to expect God to work similarly in their lives, telling them that such experiences should be normal for Christians.

A media piece that profoundly influenced many was a DVD called "The Finger of God." It showcased clips of healings, gold fillings appearing in teeth, manna with healing properties appearing, and stories of people being raised from the dead. This film introduced a growing number of UK Christians to the ministry of Bethel Church in Redding, US.

The music and teachings from Bethel strongly shaped my spiritual journey. I avidly listened to their music and read books from ministries that shared similar beliefs. The emphasis on grace was particularly comforting, with sayings like 'God is in a good mood' and 'God is good – all the time' circulating widely in the churches.

One memorable experience was attending a conference in Torquay, Devon, with Patricia King as the main speaker. She was based in the US and had a global ministry. She was accompanied by a man covered in gold dust, who shared stories of being used by God to influence powerful people in the governments of far-flung countries. He didn't travel there in the conventional way.

He was transported there supernaturally just as we read that Philip was in Acts Chapter 8.

However, the most astonishing occurrence at the conference was the miraculous appearance of gemstones. While I had heard of this phenomenon, I had never seen it myself until that day except in The Finger of God film. I videoed gemstones that a woman in the crowd found under her seat, keeping the footage on my phone to show others back at our local church.

Our local church hosted visiting speakers who encouraged us to embrace a deeper experience of the supernatural. Man and wife team Trevor and Sharon Baker brought a revival from America and wanted to impart it to our congregation. Trevor, in one instance, spoke on the church platform and asked us to picture the Holy Spirit as a football that he held in his hands. He dropped the ball and kicked it into the congregation. If the 'ball' hit someone, they would either fall, jerk violently, or be affected in some other way. Laughter filled the meeting as he ministered in a light-hearted way, encouraging us let go of 'religion' and experience God as someone to have fun with.

Another memorable visiting speaker was James Maloney from the US, who shared messages of revival and the church entering a season of powerful witness. His message was based on a book he had recently written: *The Dancing Hand of God: Unveiling the Fullness of God Through Apostolic Signs, Wonders, and Miracles.*

The Christian music album called *Angel of Awakening* was immensely popular then. The title captured the prevailing sense of anticipation, with angels believed to be rousing the church for a Great Awakening when millions would find salvation and the kingdom would manifest on Earth.

Training for Supernatural Ministry

I was committed to establishing a ministry focused on signs and wonders in my town, involving 'treasure hunting' and home group activities. This endeavour led me to participate in the inaugural Training for Supernatural Ministry (TSM) Course offered by a local church well thought of within the church stream I was a part of. It was possibly one of the first in the country.

I was a self-employed gardener then but had received a job offer as a support worker in a Christian rehab unit, which would have been a step up from my gardening work. However, I declined the job because I believed the TSM course was more significant. It required two full days per week for a year, and though my prospective employers tried to accommodate it, satisfactory arrangements couldn't be made.

The TSM Course consisted of teachings, much of which were from DVDs of sessions at the Bethel Church School of Supernatural Ministry in the US. It emphasised the idea that, since we carried a connection to God through the Holy Spirit and took Him with us wherever we went, we should see ourselves as 'little gods' capable of 'shifting the atmosphere' of the places we visited. Bill Johnson, the main speaker at Bethel Church, shared stories of how the atmosphere of a hardware store changed when he entered.

I enjoyed the opportunities to go out on the streets locally and to other towns with TSM teams to experiment with these concepts, putting into practice what I had learned about treasure hunting and praying for healing.

During the course, I had a prophetic vision that I shared in one of the sessions. I was reminded that the Christian family who had taken me in following my conversion kept chickens and that they used a homemade incubator to hatch the eggs. In my vision, I saw TSM students in an incubator, and as each 'egg' hatched, various, often strange, reptilian-looking creatures emerged. I interpreted this as a manifestation of the diverse ministries that would emerge from participating in the course and future courses. These ministries would be powerful but different from anything we had seen in Christian ministry before. I was allowed to share this vision with the students, and it was accepted as a genuine prophecy being aligned with the ethos of TSM.

A passage from Isaiah was frequently quoted to encourage us

to embrace the 'new thing' God was doing:

Forget the former things ... See, I am doing a new thing!
Now it springs up; do you not perceive it?
Is. 43: 18-19.

We were eager to see an acceleration of these ministries that would usher in the promised revival. The emphasis was on experiencing increased spiritual activity, as it was our destiny.

I listened to many messages from innovative preachers, apostles, and prophets leading the way, allowing me to discern God's direction and share prophetic insights with others. Prayers of 'activation' were a regular part of my life, with the focus on aligning ourselves with God's purposes.

The TSM course strongly encouraged us to develop any prophetic ministry we might have. At various seminars, called Father's Heart Conferences, organised by the same fellowship running TSM, students were given the opportunity to practise prophecy. Conference attendees went into side rooms where students like me would prophesy over them. Although I worried about not having anything to say, we had been taught to speak the first thing that came to mind, trusting that it was God speaking. TSM emphasised not worrying about 'getting it wrong.' Mistakes were considered part of the learning process.

Towards the end of the course, I began to receive another prophetic word building on the earlier incubator vision. It was inspired by the mood and spirit of a rock song I had known for years, in which people were encouraged to move onto a highway that would give them a fuller, more exciting life. One line in the song mentioned seeing lizzard creatures in the air, which I linked to the reptilian creatures seen earlier. The message I intended to convey was that people should move forward to be part of a powerful and innovative ministry. It wasn't the inspiration for the message that mattered but the mood and spirit behind it. This message resonated with the prevailing desire to see signs and wonders take place. I knew from the teachings on prophecy that pictures and visions could originate from various sources, and their authenticity was determined by their alignment with other prophetic voices.

I would sometimes have thoughts like this coming from things around me in my everyday experiences or from a Bible verse or passage. I would find some kind of message in such thoughts and then build upon it. If I got these thoughts in midweek, I might share them at a church homegroup or if at a weekend it would be in a Sunday meeting. I would be thinking about my "message" and add bits to it to make it seem profound often on the way to the meeting. By the time I got there and overcame the hurdles of self-doubt and a fear of speaking at the microphone in front of the congregation, I would have a credible story about something I believed God wanted to say to the church. Not all prophecies took shape this way but, looking back now, I see that, sadly, many did. If the message "fitted in" no one ever questioned the source.

As it turned out, I never had the chance to share that 'lizzard' message because, shortly afterward, God began to redirect my life entirely, dramatically altering my view of the church landscape.

After completing the TSM course, I approached the elders of my church to propose establishing a Healing on the Streets (HOTS) ministry. I had the support of a few individuals in my church and some from the TSM course to form a team, but I wanted the endorsement of the elders. After a meeting with them, they approved the idea, and in 2010, the team began going out on Saturdays in the town centre to pray for healing with members of the public.

I contacted the Vineyard Church in Coleraine, Northern Ireland, where HOTS was pioneered, for guidance on setting up this ministry. On Saturdays, our team was joined by a small group of volunteers, and, after brief instructions and a time of prayer, we went out and engaged with people of all ages and backgrounds in the town centre. This was ahead of its time, as it wasn't until 2016 that my church stream invited the founder of this ministry to speak at their annual churches gathering, the Catalyst Festival.

Shortly after launching the healing ministry, I enrolled in a School for the Prophets run by the same church that started TSM, hoping it might develop into a ministry involving church members who had been hesitant to participate. TSM-style courses and Schools of the Prophets were being introduced in other towns to stimulate interest in the supernatural. I was excited to be at the forefront of what God was doing in the church and eagerly anticipated the next steps in my journey.

However, God had other plans, which would lead me in a completely unexpected direction.

Chapter 5

RADICAL REORGANISATION

How Did I End Up Here?

In the previous chapters, I recounted my experiences as an ordinary believer within the context of church life spanning approximately four decades. The transformation from an orthodox form of Christianity to a belief system conflicting with biblical teachings is evident. Although I believed I was living a Spirit-led life in close friendship with the Lord, it became clear that I had drifted away from Him, unknowingly, due to personal struggles with besetting sins and harmful influences.

Erroneous teachings and practices, I encountered during Dales Bible weeks, New Frontiers camps, local church events, and conferences, played a significant role in leading me astray. The teachings are detrimental to spiritual growth and have created an environment within New Church organisations and the broader UK church that goes unchallenged.

However, God had a plan. He alerted me to the danger, rescued me, and brought me back into a close relationship with Him. These events are not unique to me; many believers are being alerted by similar revelations and some are responding. As you read these pages, I hope you will also ask God to open your ears to His message.

While I would never elevate any experience above my encounter with Jesus at the cross and my salvation, God's rescue plan for me bore similarities. After recognising my spiritual condition, I had to repent of my errors and recommit myself to the Lord, much like my initial conversion. This process led to a fresh discovery of biblical truths in the context of the present times.

This journey paralleled the steps I took following my conversion, aligning my life with God's requirements. In a way, it was akin to recalculating one's path during a car journey when making a wrong turn, prompted by a satnav device. It may instruct you to do a U-turn to get you back on the right road. The Lord did this with me, but only with hindsight do I see the enormity and the seriousness of this redirection.

Recalculate!

While visiting my daughter in Bexhill on the South coast, her family and my wife and I went to visit the nearby town of Rye. I set out alone earlier to capture photographs of Dungeness, a unique landscape known as 'the desert of England.' The area comprises miles of shingle beach never covered by the tide. The stones are of various colours; cream-coloured, brown, and black. While photographing old boats stranded on the shore, I realised I had dropped my car key.

The black oval key, devoid of a key ring, resembled the black stones on the beach. Panic set in as I understood there was no spare key in Bexhill or back home. The idea of finding it over thousands of square meters was overwhelming. As I prayed, I thought I may have dropped the key when taking the camera from my jacket. To have any chance of finding it, I would need to retrace my steps to the exact places I would have stood, a nearly impossible task.

Then a clear thought came to me: I could use the photographs on my digital camera to retrace my steps. By trial and error, I eventually found the key. This experience taught me the principle that to move forward, one may have to revisit the places and experiences of one's past. Sometimes, finding the key to progress means reconsidering the path taken.

God guided me to revisit my spiritual journey, even though I didn't fully understand the scope of it then. I needed to reassess my salvation and Christian life. This led me on a path of rediscovering the closeness I once had with God and regaining the healthy fear of Him that I had lost.

This transformation unfolded over the following months and years as I earnestly sought God. Initially, my quest was driven by a desire to find the truth about perplexing issues, but this led me to re-establish a deeper relationship with Him. My understanding of the Christian walk and church life had become tainted by a blend of truth and falsehood, a perilous place to remain.

What I Believed

Regrettably, I couldn't write about every experience and influence that shaped my beliefs from the late 1970s until 2017. (The end of that period was when everything changed for me). My aim is to provide an honest account of my spiritual journey without sensationalism, with a specific purpose that will become apparent later.

I wanted to explain my naivety as I embraced the signs, wonders, apostolic, and prophetic movement within the New Church environment. I want to make it clear that I was not an outsider; I was deeply involved.

Apart from the fundamental tenets of the Christian faith, (my beliefs aligned with traditional Evangelicalism), I had also adopted additional beliefs. I held the conviction that the Church would take over worldly institutions and establish the Kingdom of God on Earth through signs, wonders, healings, and the proliferation of prophetic and apostolic ministries. While leaders of the New Churches largely subscribe to these beliefs, most church members remain unaware of their origins and their prevalence in church policies.

The belief that the Old Testament had been surpassed by a superior New Testament gave credence to the idea that the Jewish people had lost significance, having been replaced by the church as the New Israel. I never consciously questioned this doctrine. The teaching I received displayed a vague indifference to factual details surrounding it and I simply went along with it.

In summary, these were my beliefs just before I was prompted to re-evaluate everything.

God-directed Change

Although my orthodox beliefs remained intact, I embarked on a process of re-evaluating all other aspects of my faith. This examination did not involve any esoteric mystical knowledge but unveiled widely known and comprehensible truths that many Christians have believed and written about over many years but in my sphere had been obscured by false teachings. The practices I and New Church congregations engaged in were not grounded in biblical truths; they entangled us in a fabricated reality that posed a serious threat to believers. The story of the children playing on a sandbank serves as an allegory to illustrate the very real danger that must not be underestimated.

My transformation began when I began questioning instead of passively accepting everything I encountered. These issues were deeply ingrained in the DNA of my church and church stream. I initially hoped to find little flaws or nuanced disagreements over a minor issue but was confronted with inconsistencies and a lack of integrity that forced me to dig deeper. It was so disturbing that I had to embark on a journey of seeking Truth to uncover what was genuine.

You might be wondering about the specific beliefs I am alluding to and why they should concern you. You might argue that you are saved, filled with the Spirit, reaching out to others, and engaged in social action, and thus don't see the need to scrutinise alleged errors. Your daily responsibilities and busyness might overshadow the importance of such investigation. However, I would assert that if it matters to God, it should matter to you, especially considering our limited time. Truth should be a priority; who wants to be fed falsehoods or have things hidden from them?

You might be wondering what issues I am referring to. If you are a member of a New Church, you might find it puzzling to hear that there are any issues with the beliefs and practices of these organisations. However, the mere puzzlement is a significant part of the problem, as will become evident.

Turning Aside to Look

This is how the Lord rescued me. He plucked me from my existing path and transplanted me into a completely different realm. It was as though He said, "Hey, come over here and take a look. You need to comprehend this; it holds great importance to Me." This event resembled the story of Moses and the burning bush. It initiated my journey of discovery.

To understand what is going on in the world everyone must start here, or rather, you should start where God had me start.

It all starts (and ends) with the matter of Israel and the Jews.

Begin Here

My journey began unintentionally with a tour to Israel in September 2017, and it had a profound effect on me.

I had always wanted to visit Israel, but I wasn't particularly sentimental about it. Being a Christian, I had heard emotional stories and accounts from people who had visited, which I found mawkish My primary curiosity lay in exploring the modern history and politics of the region, as my knowledge of Israel and its significance had become vague and irrelevant after years in non-denominational churches that seldom mentioned these topics.

The little knowledge I had left me unprepared for what I was about to discover.

You don't need to physically journey to Israel to understand the issues; you can study them independently. However, visiting the country exposed me to a significant gap between the events I witnessed, their portrayal in the global media, and how they were presented in our churches. These inconsistencies extended to Bible prophecy and the teachings in most churches. I'll explain why shortly.

During the summer of 2017, I took on some freelance media work with a Christian ministry team near my home in Bedford, UK. They organised a Study Tour of Israel for September that year. I joined the team and soon found myself filming their Bible Study sessions.

An Innocent Abroad

Picture fifty adults on a sweltering day, riding a tour bus through Israel, with about forty Americans and the rest being English. Hanna, our Israeli tour guide, captivated us with her commentary on the vast plains of agricultural abundance we were passing through.

She remarked, "You know, that's redemption. For thousands of years, they considered this place a horrific malarial swamp..."

Throughout the day, I found her comments either astonishing or alarming, or both. She often implied a divine hand behind the flourishing landscape we observed, using words like "redemption." I'd heard various debates about this, but I tried to avoid getting drawn into controversies. I had a job to do, and I needed to focus on that.

Hanna continued, "... this is really redemption... and so now, this is, as you can see, very fertile," describing how this once swampy plain had been transformed into fertile agricultural land.

We were on a modern tour bus, gliding across a flat-as-a-pancake landscape on pristine roads with shiny signs, making it seem as though everything had been completed yesterday. The Jezreel Valley in northern Israel surrounded us, with fields of melons, oranges, beans, wheat, sunflowers, cotton, and grazing sheep and cattle. In the distance, the flat terrain gave way to khaki-coloured hills that rose steeply into mountains with dark grey peaks.

As I tried to set the date on my camcorder to September 2017, Hanna was talking about the geography, "a hundred and sixty square miles," and then something that grabbed my attention, "and we're looking at the Golan Heights over there... all those bumps along the top are extinct volcanoes."

I couldn't help but wonder about the Golan Heights, a place I had heard about countless times on news channels. I thought, "Isn't that disputed territory, like much of this perplexing country?"

Arrival

I thought of our arrival earlier in the day. The Americans had met-up with the English group at Heathrow. After an overnight flight, we landed in Tel Aviv around 8 in the morning. By the time we left the airport, it was past 9, and the bright sunlight greeted us with 30-degree heat. We eagerly reached for water bottles in our backpacks after boarding the tour bus.

A taxi pulled up alongside our bus, and a woman with wild, light-brown hair emerged - Hanna. As the driver loaded her luggage, she introduced herself as our tour guide over the bus's PA system. She had a down-to-earth demeanour combined with an authoritative voice.

The tour was organised by Clifford and Monica, who led the organisation I had joined as a freelance media worker. They had hired me to do various media-related tasks and to film the talks and seminars on the tour. Later I would find myself working on the ministry's online magazine.

Before this opportunity, I had been working in London in the media team of an international charity, the Church Mission Society (CMS), until 2009 when I was made redundant. My work there included producing their flagship 24-page full colour *Yes* magazine. Working alongside a marvellously fastidious editor, I considered it a privilege to meet missionaries from all over the world, be part of interviewing them, and telling their stories.

Clifford, an ordained Minister with a PhD in sociology, had an extensive background that included lecturing at the University of London, working in Parliament, and writing over 40 books. Monica, the former Executive Officer of the British Church Growth Association and Editor of the Church Growth Digest, had also authored numerous books.

As we left the airport, we could see Tel Aviv's modern buildings and stylish hotels in the distance. Hanna provided some information about the country's size, mentioning it was about the same as Wales in the UK and slightly larger than New Jersey in the US. I wondered what all the fuss was about on the world's media when the place was so small.

Curiosity Turns to Shock

Our first tourist stop was Caesarea, an intriguing historic seaport on the Mediterranean coast. The bus parked near ancient ruins, including a stadium, more accurately a hippodrome. It was an enormous oval track with stone seating overlooking the sea. Our guide told us what went on there. I quickly got the picture. This was the place where Roman citizens used to sit enjoying the wonderful sea view as a backdrop while they watched people getting killed. Think of that old film Ben Hur or, more recently Gladiator, and you're in the right territory. Nearby were the ruins of a palace, once the base of the infamous Pontius Pilate. At the height of the Roman Empire, during the reign of the emperor Tiberius, he was the Governor of the region.

Just off the coast, Israel had discovered substantial oil and gas reserves, with pipelines coming ashore at this point. These finds will make the country self-sufficient and eventually an exporter.

Our next stop wasn't on the typical tourist route. We turned off the main road and pulled into a small coach park beside a vast compound. At first glance, I thought it was a Holocaust Museum with high barbed wire fences, watchtowers, rows of narrow huts, and imposing double gates at the entrance. An attendant was opening one of the gates, and our group disembarked. Apart from us, the place was deserted.

It was the Atlit Detainee Camp, a restored version of the historic camp built, with several others along Israel's west coast, in the 1930s. There were six or seven huts in rows but when the camp was in full use it would have been much larger and there would have been two hundred of these "residential" blocks with possibly four or five families or groups in each. Other huts were used as 'disinfection barracks' where new arrivals were stripped of their clothing and disinfected with DDT.

But who were the unfortunate inhabitants?

The camp once housed Jewish families fleeing pogroms, Nazi persecution and death camps before, during, and after World War II. Many were Holocaust survivors.

Hanna spoke about the British failure to implement a League

of Nations directive from the 1920s, which led to these Jews being considered illegal immigrants and imprisoned in these camps.

I couldn't help but feel sorry for them. Escaping the horrors of the death camps, they ended up in a place reminiscent of the concentration camps they had fought to escape from. It was confusing because I thought they weren't supposed to be here. After all, wasn't this Palestine, belonging to the Palestinians?

Hanna talked about "The British Mandate," an agreement created at a conference in San Remo, Italy in 1920, with the purpose of providing a homeland for Jewish people. I was even more puzzled. San Remo? What was all this, fake news? I decided to make notes, promising myself I'd research it when I got home.

On We Go

We reboarded the bus and headed north towards Mount Carmel. The bus climbed uphill relentlessly, and, once we reached the summit, Hanna explained the significance of the location. She led us off the bus into a courtyard.

"This is part of a mountain range, 550 meters in height, a few miles inland from the coast over there," she pointed. "We are overlooking the Jezreel Valley down there", she waved in a northerly direction. The courtyard was roughly thirty square meters with a railing around the edge. As I peered over the edge, I realised we were perched on top of a high mountain with sheer drops on nearly all sides. While Hanna continued to speak, I stood by the railing, looking down into the valley. The view was breath-taking but also made me feel intensely uneasy when close to the edge.

"This is where Elijah confronted the Prophets of Baal (see 1 Kings 18)," Hanna explained.

I turned my attention back to Hanna, who had the group gathered around her, fully engrossed in her narrative. She began to talk about the Jezreel Valley, where a significant battle would occur between Israel and the enemies of God, prophesied to take place at the end of Jesus' 1,000-year reign on Earth (see Rev. 20). Jezreel was also known as Megiddo, and the topographical name "Har Megiddo" (Mount Megiddo) is where we get the word "Armageddon."

She was saying how the Israeli Defence Forces are on constant alert because of rocket attacks from the Gaza Strip, Lebanon and Syria; and from terrorism within the country and then, as if to illustrate her point, two fighter jets flew over the mountain, coming from an air base in the valley, creating a deafening roar.

Back on the bus, Hanna began discussing our descent into and crossing of the valley. This was when she had started educating us so keenly about the "redemption".

Kibbutzniks

We crossed the valley and journeyed into the region called 'the Galilee', arriving at our first overnight stay in a Kibbutz. The simple, single-story bungalows provided basic accommodations with clean and tidy rooms that included a bedroom, a small kitchenette, a shower room, and a toilet. The more permanent residents spent most of their time outdoors.

At the large communal canteen for the evening meal, Karen announced that the planned seminar had been postponed due to everyone's fatigue. I was relieved not to be filming that evening.

Returning to my room, I reminisced about the hippie types I knew in my 20s, some of whom had become Kibbutzniks in the 1960s and 70s. Although I couldn't recall their experiences in detail, I knew they had spent time in places like this, smoked a lot of marijuana, and found it a challenging, barren land. They received free meals and lodging but had to work on the land. I wondered if some of them had stayed in the very same cabin I was in that night. I settled in for the night, put my camera on charge, and quickly fell asleep.

The next day we went up onto the Golan Heights and, passing near the border fence with Syria, saw rows of Israeli tanks guarding against potential invasion.

Over the following days, we visited most of the essential

tourist sites in Northern Israel, including the 'Jesus Triangle,' an area of a few square miles around the northern end of the Sea of Kinneret, where Jesus had conducted most of his teaching and ministry – and changed the world.

Bethsaida, a ruined city, was a disconcerting place, with enormous piles of stones scattered over the hillsides. It was one of the two cities, along with Korazin, that Jesus cursed (see Matthew 11).

The museum of the early Jewish settlers was eye-opening, displaying photographs of a land stripped of vegetation. I wondered why these pioneers had come. You might think these pioneers were high-minded visionaries but most of them didn't have any fixed ideas as to why they came. Some even dressed like cowboys, and it seemed the Arabs who sold them land had the last laugh. It looked like a desolate place.

Jerusalem

For the second half of the tour, we were booked into a hotel in Jerusalem. More up-market than the Kibbutz! On the way into the city, we passed through Judea and Samaria, now called the West Bank, with its areas designated for Arabs only, marked by "No Western, No Jews" signs. It reminded me of the ethnic enclaves I had seen in the UK towns in freelance journalists' videos, with signs like 'No Whites after 6 pm.' Contrary to popular belief, most Israelis seemed to tolerate these restrictions. In many places, Palestinians lived in upscale residential areas and impressive properties, even in the West Bank.

While we visited various sites in Jerusalem that typically appealed to tourists, I found the less-travelled places to be the most intriguing, surprising, and puzzling. At the entrances to the Temple Mount, one of the top three holy sites in Islam, armed Israeli Defence Forces ensured safe passage for Arab worshippers. It was a stark contrast to how Western media portrayed the situation, which often suggested that Israelis were preventing Arabs from visiting the site. This wasn't what I witnessed. Most Arabs appeared to feel safe and content under Israeli rule, including our "Palestinian" bus driver, who lived in a desirable part of Jerusalem.

On the penultimate day, we explored the old city of Jerusalem on foot, and on the final day, we made another quick visit before heading to the airport.

We returned and said our goodbyes at Heathrow to our American friends.

Many places we visited couldn't be covered in this account. The journey had been incredibly enlightening, and it left me with a profound challenge regarding the truth about events in that country, how they were reported, especially in Western media, and how they were viewed within the church. It was immensely curious to me.

Chapter 6

THE HUNT BEGINS

Curiouser and Curiouser

During the tour, I made extensive notes about my experiences. Once back home, I began my research, which immediately raised some pressing questions.

Why was there such a significant gap between reality and its reporting? Why had my church never addressed these issues? Did Jews have any rights in Israel, and did any of this even matter? I initially believed that a bit of online research would quickly resolve these apparent differences of opinion.

I had started editing the footage I had recorded and showed some clips to my church homegroup. I was trying to explain some of the questions brewing in my mind especially the ones about Bible prophecies relating the return of the Jews to their own land.

However, my understanding was limited at that point, and my aim was simply to convey what I had observed. But then, a member of the homegroup, someone whose opinion, I thought, would have epitomised the view of the leadership, made a remark that made me see where I and the church stood on these issues.

"Oh, but that's just Old Testament!"

This comment was revealing, highlighting the church's diminishing emphasis on the Old Testament in favour of the New Testament over the years. This shift prompted me to investigate the reasons behind it, its significance, and how it had transpired. I tried to discuss these matters with friends in the church, but I encountered strong reactions.

"Well, the Israelis are a very aggressive people, and they're trying to grab more land, aren't they?"

I attempted to counter this perspective by sharing my own observations, but enthusiastic support for Israel or the Jews in these conversations led to being thought of as a fanatic. I was bewildered by these reactions and began to question them.

Was this the prevailing view in many UK churches? The church never addressed the topic, and there appeared to be resistance to even broaching the subject. I was compelled to uncover the reasons behind this.

My initial research didn't reveal minor differences of opinion but rather deeper and wider issues that left me astounded.

Another Look at the Battle

A few months into my investigations, Karen, the UK tour organiser, invited me to a seminar on understanding the Hebrew worldview. While I found it interesting, it didn't provide answers to my questions.

A month later, another similar seminar focussing more on cultural issues was scheduled, and my interest was piqued due to my background in Cultural Studies during my journalism degree. The speaker was an author well-versed in the topics I was investigating, and I was eager to listen and took notes.

However, the seminar took an unexpected turn. The speaker shed light on various issues related to Western culture, explaining how political systems and institutions had been undermined by malevolent forces over the past century.

He discussed the ideas of Alice Bailey and the New Age movement that began in the 1920s. These demonically inspired plans, aiming to dismantle Western civilisation, had been, he said, successful.

He explained how these plans were similar, and possibly connected, to a later scheme, hatched by Marxists in the post war years. He referred to this as Postmodernism or Cultural Marxism. The primary target of these attacks on Western society are its foundations: the Judaeo-Christian roots and the family unit. I had previously studied Postmodernism during my degree when it had been presented as a positive concept, but it now appeared far less positive.

The speaker also highlighted how this had influenced Western perceptions of contemporary events in Israel. This intrigued me. Then he detailed how the neo-Marxist Liberation movements of the 1960s changed Western culture. This was enlightening for me; I began to get an inkling about what was behind the chaos I had experienced then and gave me a desire to find out more.

I have explained how, following my conversion, I had received a revelation about the devil's activities in the world, while emphasising God's love for humanity. Satan exploits humanity's inherent sinful desires due to the Fall, to fulfil his destructive goals. My understanding of these concepts deepened over time as I explored the Bible and various spiritual matters. Now I began to feel I was learning all over again but in a much more profound way. I saw the devices, the systems, the people, the organisations, and movements our enemy had used and is still using. God was beginning pull back the curtain that hides the spiritual allowing me to peek behind it.

To see how the enemy had employed such tactics in worldly institutions and societies was one thing but to discover he had been rolling out equally destructive plans for the church was particularly worrying.

It was concerning that church leaders never addressed these issues, leaving me to assume they might not even be aware of them. Yet, the larger question loomed: was this all true? The topics I was investigating were so extensive and deeply ingrained in culture that they seemed to resemble conspiracy theories with little basis in fact.

Despite my reservations, I was compelled to find out the truth.

Where I Lived and What I Lived For
When I initially started investigating, I had no idea how far-reaching and deep my journey would take me. It began casually but quickly intensified as I uncovered a multitude of issues that

were never addressed within church circles.

I had initially focused on Israel and the Jews, but it became clear that I needed to explore the matters raised by the seminar speaker as well. He obviously thought these affected the church, so I too considered them worthy of investigation. Since these issues intertwined, I sought God's guidance to untangle and reveal the truth.

Over several months, I devoted myself to studying the Bible about these matters, praying, acquiring books, and conducting online research. Wherever scriptures were quoted, I delved into Bible studies. I aimed to be like the Bereans in Acts 17, who, upon hearing the Word of God, diligently searched the scriptures daily to verify the truth. I was determined to be a Berean.

This was where I lived and what I lived for as I delved deeper to puzzle out these things. While curiosity initially led me, I was soon overwhelmed by surprise and amazement leading me to study my Bible more earnestly. The silence surrounding these issues in church meetings only fuelled my interest.

It became evident that this wasn't merely a social, political, or cultural matter; it was spiritual. This revelation raised two key points: first, God was revealing something profound to me, and second, a purely human and intellectual understanding wouldn't suffice. I had been asking God questions, but as time went on, this evolved into an intense seeking. This process involved taking extensive notes, and I began writing fragments of text outlining the information I had unearthed, even though they remained unconnected at that stage.

I intentionally refrained from consulting the organisation that had commissioned the filming; I didn't want any external influences. I needed to seek God and lay everything before Him, pleading for guidance.

Chapter 7

DISCOVERING TRUTH

During my visit to Israel, I was struck by the disparities between Western media reports and my personal observations. Equally perplexing was the silence of the church on these issues. I've mentioned some of the things that piqued my curiosity: the Atlit Detainee Camp, unfulfilled promises to protect Jewish interests, and Israeli resilience in the face of constant threats and global animosity. What captivated me the most, though, was the birth and growth of this nation, achievements in urban and infrastructure development, and agricultural blossoming since the interwar years.

The compound near the Kibbutz where I stayed had been kept as it was in the days of the early inhabitants. It features a museum that vividly depicts the hardships faced by those early Jewish pioneers.

Before we dive deeper into my quest for truth, it's essential to acknowledge my previous understanding of the Israel-Palestine situation, as shaped by Western mainstream media: a narrative that paints Israelis as aggressors who occupy foreign land, bullying the Palestinians. It alleges that any dissent is met with ruthless force from the Israeli Defence Forces, a lie perpetuated by a media manipulated by sinister influences.

I discovered that modern Israel is far from the 'illegal occupier' state it is routinely made out to be in the Western media. I used to believe the lies about Israel, as many others do, but it has every legal right to exist under international law, and much of what circulates about it is either untrue or grossly distorted.

In wanting to untangle the perplexities surrounding this issue, I studied the history of the region. What I discovered was remarkable.

A Brief History of Israel and the Jews

If you read your Bible, you know that God brought Israel into existence, starting with the call and covenant with Abraham and later through promises to his descendants. The land and the people are inseparable in these covenants, emphasised by over 170 references to the land promised to Abraham and his offspring.

I will not major on Old Testament history here but move forward to 63 BC when Jerusalem and the region was reorganised as a Roman Province called Judea. The Judeans staged several revolts against the Roman Empire leading to their suppression and a ban on Jewish access to Jerusalem in 132 AD. They were forced to scatter across the known world – or face death. Emperor Hadrian then renamed the region Palestina, an intentional insult to the Jews, referring to the Philistines, long-time enemies of the Israelites.

The current diaspora is a temporary one. Jesus said that Jerusalem would fall, that Jews would be scattered over all the earth and that Jerusalem would be trodden down by the Gentiles, until the times of the Gentiles are fulfilled (see Luke 21).

It is not, as some say, a final rejection by God of his chosen people but, because he dearly loves them, he must discipline them just as he does you and me. Bible prophecies show how, in his mercy, he promises to bring his people back to the land of Israel and bless them there.

The times of the Gentiles are coming to an end. These prophetic promises are being fulfilled before our eyes today.

Deserted

From the 4th century onwards the land that had been renamed Palestina was under the rule of the Byzantine Empire.

Jews were regarded as second-class citizens throughout the Empire which comprised the eastern half of the previous Roman

Empire while the western half, all the countries of present-day Europe, was taken over by the Ottoman Turks.

In the 16th century the region then called Palestine was under the domination of the Islamic Ottoman Empire but its decline in the 19th century saw the increasing influence of the European powers there.

Explorations of the region in 1865, under the patronage of Queen Victoria, discovered a land neglected and underpopulated. Accounts of other groups who travelled there describe a land that was bleak and abandoned.

In 1869, Mark Twain published *The Innocents Abroad*, a travel book in which the American author records his observations on journeys through various European countries and an eventual excursion through the Holy Land. Twain became frustrated by the primitiveness of the settlements and roads he encountered. He describes the landscape as dreary, repulsive, bare and rocky and wrote that even trees and shrubs that might grow in poor soil, such as the olive and the cactus, were virtually non-existent there.

His unflattering remarks reveal:

The Dead Sea and the Sea of Galilee sleep in the midst of a vast stretch of hill and plain wherein the eye rests upon no pleasant tint, no striking object, no soft picture dreaming in a purple haze or mottled with the shadows of the clouds. Every outline is harsh, every feature is distinct, there is no perspective - distance works no enchantment here. It is a hopeless, dreary, heart-broken land.[1]

In another nearby region he makes similar observations:

There is not a solitary village throughout its whole extent - not for thirty miles in either direction. There are two or three small clusters of Bedouin tents, but not a single permanent habitation. One may ride ten miles, hereabouts, and not see ten human beings.[2]

The Balfour Declaration

The Ottoman Empire joined forces with the Austro-Hungarian

Empire and Germany against France, Russia, and the British Empire at the outbreak of WW1. The British assembled troops to combat this alliance.

Palestine was already witnessing an influx of Jews escaping rising anti-Semitism in Europe and the Russian pogroms. This saw the beginning of the Zionist movement led by Theodor Herzl, who aimed to establish a Jewish homeland in Palestine.

Various leaders in the region held discreet discussions about the post-war scenario but no agreements they made had any legal binding.

Meanwhile, David Lloyd George had become Prime Minister of Britain, with Lord Arthur Balfour as his Foreign Secretary. The new government considered the concerns of the Zionists and the plight of Jews across Europe, stemming from events as far back as 1349. The history of persecutions, massacres, pogroms, and expulsions in various countries weighed heavily on their minds. In collaboration with the US, France, and Italy, they decided to support the Zionist idea of a Jewish homeland. As soon as they did this, everything changed.

British and allied forces struggling to wrest Palestine from the Turks and secure the strategic Suez Canal quickly secured a significant military victory in the campaign. Soon after, the Turks surrendered to the allies followed by the capitulation of the Germans and the Austro-Hungarian Empire.

In October 1917, a committee of ministers convened to draft what would later become known as The Balfour Declaration.[3]

The Declaration had the full support of the allied powers and, contrary to popular belief today, also had the support of Arab leaders at the time. It was a promise to enable and assist the formation of a national homeland for the Jewish people in Palestine. At that time, it was simply a political statement of intent with no legal authority in international law.

Woodrow Wilson, the US President at the time, issued what become known as the 'Fourteen Points'[4], part of which stressed a need for sovereignty, security, and autonomous development for the Turkish portion of the Ottoman Empire.

Wilson's fourteen points became generally accepted by other nations following the end of the War. The ideas driving these points were those that would later form the aims of League of Nations, which had been established by the Paris Peace Conference of 1919 and the Treaty of Versailles.

At these gatherings, the supreme powers had invited both Arab and Jewish leaders to make their territorial claims.

These initial agreements were legally binding.

San Remo

The post-war conference of the Allied Supreme Council convened in April 1920, in the Italian Riviera town of San Remo. Attended by the four Principal Allied Powers of World War I, it comprised the Prime Ministers of Britain, France, Italy, and Japan's Ambassador, with America as observers.

The conference aimed to determine the future of the Middle East following the Ottoman Empire's collapse. Historically, victors in legitimate wars had the right to acquire conquered territories, but in line with Woodrow Wilson's fourteen points, the victorious allies steered clear of acquiring new colonies. Instead, they aspired to establish sovereign states over time, acknowledging that not all Middle Eastern areas were ready for full independence. Thus, they established Mandates for each territory, entrusting one of the Allied Powers with its administration—a sacred trust under the League of Nations.

Mandates were set up for Lebanon, Syria, Mesopotamia (now Iraq), and Palestine. The first three would be assisted to create systems of government and eventually rule themselves.

Palestine was to become a homeland for the Jewish people and, given that most of them were not yet living there, the Mandate for Palestine was completely different from the others. It outlined how the Land was to be inhabited until a time when Jews could form a viable nation.

Instead of being simply a geographical area, for the first time in history, Palestine became a legal entity as The Balfour Declaration was recognised and incorporated into international law. The San Remo Agreement was included in the Treaty of Sevres and confirmed by the Council of the League of Nations in July 1922. Therefore, transfer of entitlement to Palestine cannot be revoked, either by the League of Nations or the United Nations – as its successor – unless the people of Palestine want to give it up. The Arabs gained equivalent legal rights in Lebanon, Syria, and Mesopotamia.

Sovereignty over Palestine was vested in the Jewish people, and they became beneficiaries of the Land, because of their historical connection to it. Britain was assigned as the Mandatory Power.

It is very clear from the establishment of these accords that the Jewish State draws its legal existence from the San Remo Agreement of 1920, and not any later plans initiated by the United Nations. All League of Nations members supported this Agreement.

Notes:

[1] Twain, M. (1869) *The Innocents Abroad*, Ware, Hertfordshire, (this edition 2010) by Wordsworth Editions Limited, p396.

[2] Ibid, p311.

[3] https://en.wikipedia.org/wiki/Balfour Declaration (and other locations in the Public Domain).

[4] https://en.wikipedia.org/wiki/Fourteen_Points (and other locations in the Public Domain).

Chapter 8

BREAKING PROMISES

The Boundaries of the Land

On my tour of Israel, I learned it was about the size of Wales. But what were the sizes of the other mandated regions?

Lebanon, Syria, Mesopotamia, and Palestine, total nearly 744,000 square kilometers. Of this, only around 22,000 square kilometers make up the current State of Israel.

The Eastern boundary was originally defined by Arab and Jewish leaders in an agreement prior to San Remo, which included some of the East bank of the Jordan. However, Britain decided that the border should be the Jordan River itself. Mesopotamia, later Iraq, included the area now known as Jordan. Britain temporarily controlled it under a separate mandate, calling it Trans-Jordan, until it gained independence in 1946, changing its name.

The Mandate for Palestine has seen no revisions since 1947, making its stipulations applicable to the entire land west of the Jordan River, including the areas that are today referred to as the West Bank and the Gaza Strip.

Is the British Mandate Obsolete?

The League of Nations disbanded after World War II, transferring its responsibilities to the United Nations (UN). In 1947, Britain ended its stewardship of the Mandate, notifying the UN. The Mandate itself wasn't terminated, only Britain's stewardship. Similarly, Britain terminated its stewardship of the Trans-Jordan Mandate in the previous year as the country gained independence.

With the loss of the land claimed along the east bank of the Jordan, the Jews faced another potential setback. The UN proposed a Partition Plan, suggesting an Arab state, a Jewish state, and an international zone, which would include Jerusalem. This was a recommendation, not a binding directive. Nevertheless, the recommendation was accepted by the Jewish leadership but rejected by the Arabs. Once it had been rejected it had no legal validity. This appears to have sown seeds of agitation that brought problems later.

The Fulfilment of the Mandate
The Mandate for Palestine was fulfilled when the State of Israel was declared in May 1948, as anticipated by the writers of the San Remo Agreement nearly thirty years earlier. The UN officially recognised Israel's declaration when it accepted that country into membership in May 1949.

The War of Independence
Immediately after declaring independence, Israel was attacked by five neighboring Arab nations. Israel lost some of its territory in the conflict: the Golan Heights to Syria, Judea and Samaria, and part of Jerusalem, to Trans-Jordan, and the Gaza Strip to Egypt. Acquiring territory by unjustly attacking another country is prohibited by international law. Syria and Egypt occupied their captured territories, but Trans-Jordan went further, completely taking over Judea and Samaria, naming it the West Bank to connect it with the East Bank of the Jordan. Only Britain and Pakistan endorsed this annexation out of all the countries of the world, but this did not change the fact that Trans-Jordan's acquisition of the land was illegal.

Academic researcher, James E. Patrick in his study *British Christian History and the Jewish People* notes:

During and after this 1948-1949 war, Jewish refugees from Arab lands flooded into Israel, whereas equivalent numbers of Palestinian Arab refugees were denied citizenship in neighbouring countries, formally by the Arab League in

1959, to exploit the miseries of their camps indefinitely as a propaganda weapon against Israel.[1]

The Six Day War

The war of June 1967 resulted in the recapture of territories Israel had lost in 1948. This was a defensive war because Egypt had already declared war on Israel by blocking the Straits of Tiran in the Gulf of Aqaba, a strategic waterway for Israel. Similarly, shortly after the war began, Jordan also declared war on Israel after colluding with President Nasser of Egypt.

So, what happened during those momentous six days?

On May 15, while the nation celebrated its independence, Israel received news that Egypt was preparing to attack. Other Arab forces – Syria, Jordan, and Iraq, went on a war footing, ready to invade Israel.

The UN, which had been acting as a peace force in the Sinai, was told by Egypt to leave and meekly withdrew.

The Egyptians closed the Straits of Tiran to Israeli vessels while, in the north, Syria took to their vantage points on the Golan Heights and began shelling Israel.

In his article *Miracles of the Six-Day War*, D. Thomas Lancaster describes the Israelis' distress and alarm. Confronting the joint forces of Egypt, Jordan, Syria, and Iraq brought fear. The combined Arab armies had double the troops, twice the number of tanks, and four times the number of aircraft compared to Israel.

Lancaster states:

The Arab nations gleefully anticipated the coming massacre. The president of Iraq declared, "The existence of Israel is an error which must be rectified. This is our opportunity to wipe out the ignominy which has been with us since 1948. Our goal is clear—to wipe Israel off the map."[2]

The Israelis prepared solemnly for a major onslaught, readying hospitals and designating entire national parks as cemeteries for expected casualties. A mood of fear and despair hung over the nation, as the dream of a Jewish state seemed on the verge of being extinguished.

Some people spoke gloomily of what might happen, but a few others predicted God's intervention and a great victory.

Although they might be interspersed with spells of relative 'peace' and periods of intense fighting, history records that many wars continue for long periods of time. Typically, they take place over months, years and, occasionally, decades, but in 1967, over the course of a mere six days, our understanding of these things had to be redefined. Not only was this war mystifyingly swift but those six days moved the world on in the plan of God.

An article in an Israeli magazine in 2019, by the writer M. Taragin, gives some insights into the significance of this miraculous event. He writes that, since the astonishing military triumph of Israel in a war that they had no hope of winning, there has been an appalling historical revisionism of the event. The narrative, recast over many years now, that this was about territorial acquisition could not be further from the truth.

Taragin points out that Israel's military victory not only averted a potential disaster but also secured an unthinkable military triumph and created a psychological deterrent against continued Arab attacks. Importantly it also:

... reinforced Israel's diplomatic position and in particular launched Israel's crucial strategic relationship with the USA.[3]

He states that, without even mentioning their national return to Jerusalem and parts of their Biblical homeland, the military victory was enough cause for celebration. And these events resounded throughout the international community.

He goes on to say that the Jews' return in 1948 wasn't, in some ways, as significant internationally. He describes how it partly resolved the practical refugee crisis and eased the world's guilt over the Holocaust.

However, when Jews returned to Jerusalem and to the hinterland of Jewish history in Judea and Samaria, the world noticed – and trembled – at this reunion between Jews and Jerusalem, and the reintroduction of the Jewish people into history.

He emphasises what these events conveyed:

The events of 1967 signalled the restoration of historical relevance to the Jews and an indication that history was beginning to hurdle forward. After close to 2000 years' operating on the margins of history, Jews were returned - front and center - to the historical stage.[4]

The Ongoing Hostility.

The Yom Kippur War of 1973 marked a significant escalation in Arab-Israeli conflict since the 1948 War of Independence. Initiated on the holiest day of the Jewish calendar, the Day of Atonement, the conflict caught Israel by surprise as Egypt and Syria launched attacks without warning, preventing an orderly mobilisation of reserves.

Egyptian forces swiftly crossed the Suez Canal, securing its eastern bank, while Syrian forces advanced into the Golan Heights, nearing the Sea of Galilee. However, the Israeli Defence Forces (IDF) mounted a rapid counterattack, regaining territory along the Suez Canal and threatening Syrian airfields near Damascus. Despite initial reluctance, both Egypt and Syria eventually accepted a ceasefire.

The standout performer of the conflict was the Israeli Navy, which achieved notable success without suffering any losses, sinking 34 enemy vessels, and securing the country's coastline.

Despite the remarkable reversal of fortunes by the IDF, the Yom Kippur War was considered a failure in Israel's history due to the initial surprise attack, resulting in nearly 2,700 Israeli fatalities.

In 1976, the IDF conducted a daring rescue operation in Entebbe, Uganda, freeing Jewish and Israeli hostages held by Palestinian and West German militants aboard a hijacked Air France liner. Despite casualties among the rescuers and hostages, the operation was a success, significantly boosting Israeli morale.

In 1978, Palestinian terrorist organisations, based in Lebanon due to the weak central government's inability to prevent their establishment, carried out a deadly raid on civilian buses near Tel Aviv. In response, the IDF launched Operation Litani, targeting terrorist bases in Lebanon, although its impact was short-lived.

Since then, there has been a constant barrage of attacks from various terrorist organisations based in the country or in neighbouring states. These groups are often funded by Iran who have consistently advocated for the destruction of Israel as a significant element in their discourse against the nation.

The events surrounding Israel's independence and its subsequent victories against its aggressors has encountered a devious twisting and rewriting of historical fact to give the illusion that these were simply land-grabbing exercises. These events were not land-grabbing, and they were not, as some have claimed, illegal.

Illegally Occupied Territory?

Roy Thurley, a writer, and lecturer on these issues, explains there are at least two reasons why Israel's recapturing of the territories it lost in 1948 was not illegal. As part of the fulfillment of the Mandate for Palestine, these territories rightfully belonged to Israel. Thurley clarifies the issue by pointing out they were simply reclaiming what was already theirs. Israel did not acquire territory as an aggressor but in a defensive war prompted by surrounding Arab nations. After returning the Sinai Peninsula to Egypt in the peace agreement of March 1979, Israel's territory closely matched the boundaries outlined in the Mandate for Palestine. Later, Israel withdrew from the Gaza Strip in September 2005, though it did not transfer control to any other state. Consequently, legally, the Gaza Strip remains part of Israel's territory, although it is not currently occupied by them.

Thurley continues: ... It should be obvious from all this that the expression *"illegally occupied territory"* is totally inapplicable to Israel's presence in, for example, Judea and Samaria (the 'West Bank'). A state cannot 'illegally occupy' a *territory that belongs to it in the first place!* [5]

In the Bible, we see that God granted to the Jewish people an area much bigger than the land now comprising the State of Israel (including the West Bank and Gaza). For those who believe the Bible, this is enough. For those who do not view God's word as sufficient there are also these legal reasons for this entitlement they should consider.

My curiosity about the land of Israel and who it belonged to had initially been aroused by the startling comments made at the Atlit Detainee Camp. I checked out what the tour guide said about the plight of Jews entering and settling in the Holy Land at that time and uncovered the disturbing tale. Under the Mandate, Britain was supposed to oversee the settlement of Jews in the region. However, due to international pressure, particularly regarding Arab oil interests, they failed to fulfil their promise and actively obstructed immigration. Only a small number of immigrants were permitted entry, while those exceeding the quotas were considered illegal immigrants. The British employed a massive naval and military force to turn back the refugees. The displaced persons came from many parts of the world but mainly from Europe at the end of WW2. They came on the roads and on trains but mainly on the hundreds of ships sailing along the Mediterranean.

One incident that changed indifference toward their plight involved the *Exodus 1947*. The story of this ship carrying 4,515 holocaust survivors was brought to international attention by journalist Ruth Gruber who documented their deportation back to Germany. This deepened sympathy for the plight of the Jews and rallied some support for the idea of a Jewish state but, nevertheless, by the end of the blockade, hundreds of thousands had been sent back to countries from which they had fled.

Some were sent back into Europe or other parts of the world like Cyprus. The ones not deported were imprisoned in places like Atlit. About 50,000 people ended up in camps and more than 1,600 drowned at sea.

I had started to see some answers to the questions I had

regarding the presence of Jews in that region at that point in history but what about the other part of the question that had figured so prominently for me back in the Atlit Detainee Camp: the people called the Palestinians?

I had promised myself that I would investigate all these things but up to this point in my research I had not found any evidence of a so-called Palestinian people. They just didn't figure at all in my investigations. What I found instead was the fabrication of a narrative by groups of people, mainly Arabs, whose aim was to destroy the nation of Israel and even the *idea* of the nation of Israel. Others who had been taken in by this story seemed to be ready to endorse it. I must be careful to distinguish between there not being an identifiable people group called the Palestinians, and there being real people with real wants and needs.

There is a large people group who have been and are being manipulated by forces beyond themselves. As Christians, we must speak out against the system rather than the individuals caught up in it. These people need our prayers.

Grand Deceptions

Amir Tsarfati, a former major in the IDF now a speaker and writer on Israeli issues, outlines how the nations have been deceived about Israel and the Jewish people. We have seen how the land was desolate and sparsely populated. Tsarfati defines the reason for the transformation:

The only reason it is what it is today is because of God's blessing upon the work of the Jewish people.[6]

He points out that the upholding of the name Palestine and the belief that the Arabs were resident in the land first are both parts of a deceitful strategy to turn the world against Israel.

One of the key leaders of the Palestine Liberation Organisation (PLO) admitted in a newspaper interview in March 1977 [7] that the "Palestinian state" was a device to fight against Israel and bring Arab unity.

Howard Grief writes about this manufactured people group

in his extended study of the modern State of Israel[8] saying that the alleged existence of a distinct Palestinian People is nothing but an absolute fiction and fabrication which has fooled practically the whole world. If any corroborating evidence is needed, he says we should look to one of the propagators of the lie, Zuhair Muhsin, formerly a member of the executive committee of the "Palestine Liberation Organization" and the leader of the Syrian-sponsored terrorist organization aJ-Sa-'iqa (Arabic: lightning).

The truth came out in the 1977 interview this P.L.O. executive gave in which he admitted that a Palestinian people does not exist. He acknowledged that the push for a Palestinian state is a strategic part of the struggle against Israel and for Arab unity. He explained that, because former Israeli Prime Minister Golda Meir denied the existence of a Palestinian people, he had wanted to assert the opposite, claiming that there is a difference between Palestinians and Jordanians. However, he also admitted that, in reality, there is no significant difference between Jordanians, Palestinians, Syrians, and Lebanese, as all belong to the Arab people. He went on:

"It is only for political reasons that we carefully stress our Palestinian identity; for it is in the national interest of the Arabs to encourage a separate Palestinian identity to counter Zionism. Yes, the existence of a separate Palestinian identity serves only tactical purposes."[9]

This is a clear admission that the founding of a Palestinian state is a tool or expedient in the continuing battle against Israel and for Arab unity.

Grief explains how this false idea gained traction. Following the Six-Day War, Israel recovered occupied parts of the Jewish National Home in Judea and Samaria and Gaza. This left the approximately one million Arabs who lived in those regions cut off from their previous rulers, and their status uncertain.

Following a reorganisation of the P.L.O. under a new leader, Yasser Arafat, these people groups, most of whom were Jordanian citizens or those considered stateless refugees, were only too happy to take on the name, and political identity of "Palestinians".

In another place he states:

Up to the time of the creation of the State of Israel on May 15, 1948, there was no distinct nation known as "Palestinians" in existence, nor is there truly such a nation even today. This is evidenced by the fact that three key components of nationhood are missing to validate the existence of a Palestinian nation: a past history, a common language and a distinctive culture with its own national literature, traditions and customs, which differ in any significant respect from the Arabs of Syria, Lebanon, Jordan and Iraq.[10]

The notion that resistance to Israel's alleged occupation of the 'Palestinian territories' has led to the creation of a distinct 'Palestinian nation' is questionable. Rather, the Arabs of former Mandated Palestine have not engaged primarily in 'resistance' but in acts of terrorism, which began not with the alleged occupation of Judea, Samaria, and Gaza, but in the late nineteenth century when Jews began returning to their ancestral homeland in significant numbers.

Furthermore, before this period in history, as some of my earlier study showed me, not once in the books or the culture of the ancient world does the word "Palestinian" ever appear as a proper noun to describe a nation of that name or an individual member of such a nation.

Grief and Tsarfati both tell how the Palestinian problem is simply an international con game supported by liberal international nations and organisations such as the UN. The prejudice of the UN can be clearly seen through the actions of their Relief and Works Agency by which many Palestinian families get benefits comparable to, and often more, than the average annual salary in Lebanon. Tsarfati is not surprised by the effect:

...this is causing many more Arabs to register as refugees as part of an international pseudo-social welfare program.[11]

Since its independence in 1948, Israel has been subjected

to numerous attacks from Arab nations aiming to destroy it. Tsarfati argues that the Palestine Liberation Organization (PLO), founded in 1964, has been the voice and enforcer of the Palestinians' cause. According to him, their goal is not the commonly stated aim of liberating the "Palestinians" but rather something quite different:

the PLO's ultimate desire, as stated in their mandate, is to destroy what they consider to be the illegitimate nation of Israel.[12]

He refutes the notion that peace would be achieved simply by the Israelis withdrawing from disputed territories. The Palestinians, he asserts, do not seek just a portion of the land; they desire all of it. Moreover, such a "solution" has already been attempted and failed. In 2005, Israel withdrew from the Gaza Strip in a process marked by heartache. Israeli soldiers were ordered to clear Jewish homes and demolish them, causing tears among both homeowners and soldiers. Hundreds of homes, initially built with government approval, were destroyed. He appeals to us to take notice of what followed:

What did Israel receive in return for this act? Peace? Calm? Friendship?

Try rockets, missiles, mortars, and tunnels of terror.[13]

Furthermore, I discovered that some politicians, religious leaders, and educators in predominantly Arab areas of Israel intentionally exacerbate tensions through their actions. In the Gaza Strip, the West Bank, and the Old City of Jerusalem, children and young people are taught that the Balfour Declaration was illegal and that all of Israel belongs to the Arab people now known as the Palestinians.

A group of historians and international lawyers created the documentary film *Whose Land?* which challenges the claims of Palestinians who argue that the Jewish people have no historical ties to Jerusalem. These claims extend to accusations that the Jewish presence in Jerusalem is illegal and that there is an effort to Judaise the city. Alarmingly, the documentary highlights that this perspective is gaining traction in the Western world.

To summarise: the concept of a "Palestinian" nation is unfounded. Historically, an Arab nation called "Palestine" did not exist, and the adoption of the name "Palestinian" is a deceptive strategy aimed at undermining and attacking the existence of Israel. This approach emerged during Israel's founding in 1948, but those promoting this modern narrative may not realise it has deeper, more sinister roots. See Psalm 83, particularly verse 4:

"Come," they say, "let us destroy them as a nation, so that Israel's name is remembered no more."

Overview of this chapter.

My brief history of Israel and the Jews is not intended to be an exhaustive study of the subjects it touches on. To get more information study the referenced material. Also, pray, seek God in humility, and ask for the truth to be revealed to you.

When I visited the Atlit Detainee Camp in Israel, questions arose, and I promised to investigate. In writing, I assume the reader has average knowledge of Biblical history and moved to more recent events.

I showed how the region remained largely deserted until the early 1900s. I explored the Balfour Declaration and its incorporation into international law via the 1920 San Remo Agreement, allowing for a Jewish homeland in Palestine.

I detailed the events surrounding the creation of Israel in 1948 and its UN recognition in 1949. I highlighted Britain's failure to fulfill its duties as outlined in the San Remo Agreement.

I described an animosity that arose quite suddenly from surrounding nations immediately after Israel's Declaration of Independence – one that has continued up to this day. I believe that this satanically inspired animosity came via neo-Marxist influences, and I drew connections to other 'liberation' movements of that period. This is evidenced by outright war or wars, by terrorism and by media campaigns – now global – that seek to promote a narrative that is contrary to the truth. This includes the creation of a fake nation and victim group called "the Palestinians".

A basic systematic study of the historical events surrounding the creation of the State of Israel will reveal how it came about and why there is such strong opposition to it. Initially, the opposition may seem rooted in socio-political issues, but a closer examination reveals the spiritual battle at its core.

The rebirth of the nation of Israel was the eye-opener for me when I visited that country in 2017. I wondered why this isn't discussed in local churches. The reason is a harmful doctrine, known as Replacement Theology, that ignores or dismisses Israel's significance. I encourage you to research this issue and not accept church leaders' positions without question.

The land of Israel and God's people are bound up with one another. This is obvious from the scriptures especially ones relating to the Covenants. Generations of believers have had their eyes blinded by this evil doctrine. If you believe in Replacement Theology, then the land of Israel and what happens to it has no significance in our modern day but if you believe that God is a God who keeps his promises then you must take a very different view.

I will now go on to explain what I discovered by researching this issue for myself. You should not accept the position that church leaders support – either directly or by their silence on certain viewpoints – believing that they have 'done it all for us' so we don't need to be bothered with it.

I encourage you to conduct your own research. Become a Berean. Read, pray, cry out to God for truth. Ask and you will receive. Test everything by scripture. And do not be fearful. If you are a true believer who seeks to be led by Jesus, then you have no reason to fear.

I submit that God wants to make it clear to us as individuals, churches, and church streams that Israel and the Jewish people are very dear to him. His purposes for the world, both now and in the age to come, are inextricably linked to them. The churches in the Western world have placed themselves under a curse by not recognising this and by embracing Replacement Theology.

Because they do not have a love of the truth God is sending a delusion upon them so that they increasingly believe other things that are not true. I urge you, dear reader, to not be tricked by this false teaching. Read on to investigate it and start to discover its roots and its effects.

Notes:

[1] Patrick, J.E. (2017), *British Christian History and the Jewish People*, Grove Books, Cambridge, p22.

[2] Lancaster, D.T. (2017), *Miracles of the Six-Day War*, in *Messiah Magazine* at: https://ffoz.org/discover/messiah-magazine/miracles-of-the-six-day-war.html

[3] Taragin. M. (2019), *The Two Miracles of 1967*, in *The Jewish Weekly*.com at: https://thejewishweekly.com/the-two-miracles-of-1967/

[4] Ibid

[5] Thurley, R. (2010), *90 Years On: Legal Aspects of Jewish Rights in the Mandate for Palestine*, CFI Charitable Trust, Eastbourne, p9.

[6] Tsarfati, A. (2018), *The Last Hour: An Israeli Insider Looks at the End Times*, Baker Publishing Group, Michigan (p107).

[7] An interview given to James Dorsey, the Middle East affairs expert of the Dutch daily, *Trouw*, on March 31st, 1977.

[8] Grief, H. (2015), *The Legal Foundation and Borders of Israel under International Law*, Publisher, City, p516

[9] Ibid, p516

[10] Ibid, p485

[11] Tsarfati, A. (2018), *The Last Hour: An Israeli Insider Looks at the End Times*, Baker Publishing Group, Michigan, p106.

[12] Ibid, p108

[13] Ibid, p109

Chapter 9

REPLACEMENT THEOLOGY

Sleeping With the Enemy

In essence, Replacement Theology, also called Fulfillment Theology, posits that the nation of Israel, the land of Israel, and being Jewish hold no relevance today because the Church has taken the place of Israel as the People of God. The Church is seen as the new Israel. A basic examination of the subject of Israel and the Jewish people reveals a significant amount of deception prevailing in Western churches. It's not necessarily a deliberate act of deception by church leaders; rather, they themselves are so deeply entrenched in this teaching, a mixture of truth and falsehood, that they often fail to recognise it as such.

Regrettably, many ordinary churchgoers remain unaware that Replacement Theology serves as a tool of the enemy, undermining God's plans. My deepest concern is for these individuals, and that's why I've written this account of my discoveries hoping to bring awareness of the truth.

I empathise with the younger generations in the church and our brothers and sisters who have come from other nations, who often inherit this legacy of false teaching handed to them from other church members and leaders who should know better. These believers might not even be familiar with these concepts. Much like several generations of animals born in captivity they may not realise their captivity. There's a possibility that some church leaders prefer it this way.

More Digging

To delve deeper into this topic, I revisited the teachings I had absorbed over many years in various Christian settings. The sermons delivered at the Dales Bible Weeks in the 1980s and later at the New Frontiers Stoneleigh Bible Weeks had greatly influenced and motivated me. I had wholeheartedly believed in these teachings. However, I began to question the truth of them.

The Bible verses used promoted a Replacement Theology perspective:

A person is not a Jew who is one only outwardly ... No, a person is a Jew who is one inwardly ... by the Spirit and not the written code. (Rom 2.28 – 29).

These verses were used to argue that the people of God were no longer the Jews but rather Christians, rendering Jewish identity irrelevant. However, these preachers seldom went on to read the connected verses:

What advantage, then, is there in being a Jew, or what value is there in circumcision? Much in every way! First of all, the Jews have been entrusted with the very words of God.
(Rom 3.1-2).

Closely intertwined with Replacement Theology teaching was another false concept known as Restorationism, which gained prominence around then. I have written about how I became indoctrinated by these ideas in Chapter 3.

One of the passages used to promote this false teaching comes from Isaiah 60:1-5:

Arise, shine; for your light has come, And the glory of the LORD has risen upon you. "For behold, darkness will cover the earth And deep darkness the peoples; But the LORD will rise upon you And His glory will appear upon you. "Nations will come to your light, And kings to the brightness of your rising. "Lift up your eyes round about and see; They all gather together, they come to you. Your sons will come from afar, And your daughters will be carried in the arms. "Then you will see and be radiant, And your heart will thrill and rejoice; Because the abundance of the sea will be turned to you, The wealth of the nations will come to you.

To say, as we were told, that the wealth of the nations would come into the church was a misinterpretation. In reading the surrounding passages we see it is addressed to Zion, a name, in this context, for the city of Jerusalem. The straightforward meaning of these verses – relating to the importance of Jerusalem in Jesus's 1000-year reign on earth following his physical return (see Revelation 20:1-7) – was often skewed to fit the false narrative of the church's growing influence in the world. I realise we need to be aware that there may be ways God uses such verses to speak to the Church, or individuals in it. But we also need to read these Old Testament prophecies to understand their obvious meanings, and not purely spiritualise them, allegorise them, or take them out of context. This is what happened as teachers read their own ideas and prejudices into their interpretation of Holy Scripture.

With so many references to a millennial reign popping up in my investigations I felt obliged to study them carefully. In doing so it became untenable to believe that this era was *not* going to take place as church leaders taught us.

I was deceived by these misconstrued ideas, where scriptures were twisted to align with the prevailing view. Over time, this perspective led to a distorted interpretation of the Bible in which the Old Testament was downplayed. Teachers of these ideas typically skimmed over the early chapters of Genesis, moved to the New Testament for the Redemption story, and hastened toward the Consummation story—the heavenly Jerusalem.

One leader in my church made a telling remark during a sermon around the time I was investigating these matters. He commented on the US President's decision in December 2017 to recognise Jerusalem as the capital of Israel. He stated that we are not seeking an earthly Jerusalem but a heavenly one. While this statement holds true (the heavenly Jerusalem is prophesied to appear but only after Jesus's 1000-year reign), the remark highlighted the widespread ignorance about the significance of Jerusalem and of Israel in God's end-time purposes.

As previously discussed, the Bible clearly establishes that God brought Israel into existence, and the land and people of

Israel are intertwined. The land was promised to the Jews as a covenant between them and God, often with an oath.

This remains important even for Gentiles. For, if we can't trust the Lord over his promises and covenants to Israel, then surely it makes it difficult for us to trust him over his promises and covenant with us regarding our salvation.

About his enduring love for his chosen people God declares:
This is what the LORD says, he who appoints the sun to shine by day, who decrees the moon and stars to shine by night, who stirs up the sea so that its waves roar-- the LORD Almighty is his name: "Only if these decrees vanish from my sight," declares the LORD, "will Israel ever cease being a nation before me." declares the LORD.
(Jeremiah 31.35-36)

As part of the Abrahamic Covenant God says some strong words about the Jewish people:
I will bless those who bless you, and whoever curses you I will curse; and all peoples on earth will be blessed through you.(Gen. 12.3).

With scriptures like these in mind we need to be careful how we handle the issue of Israel and the Jews.

God has been explicit about His intentions regarding the land and people. Speaking through the prophet he says:
I will gather all nations and bring them down to the Valley of Jehoshaphat. There I will put them on trial for what they did to my inheritance, my people Israel, because they scattered my people among the nations and divided up my land. (Joel 3.2).

This is precisely what we see happening today as nations interfere in Israeli politics and propose "two-state solutions" hoping to avoid conflict.

Does it Matter?

Some may argue that the issues I raise here do not matter because they are not about salvation. Many fellowships make church planting and evangelism a priority, and it is not wrong to do that, but these are not the only things that the Bible and our faith are concerned with. Other things are important to God and play a role in shaping our understanding of His character and His ways. Although not directly tied to salvation, these issues can impact God's blessings and are increasingly crucial as we approach the end times, with Christ's second coming drawing near and deception on the rise.

Clinging to false teachings such as Replacement Theology can distort personal theology and worldview. Maintaining this stance may leave individuals unprepared for future challenges. In these last days, we must seek all the blessings available to us. Adhering to this incorrect doctrine will hinder that.

Malcolm Hedding, Executive Director-Emeritus of the International Christian Embassy in Jerusalem (ICEJ), has extensively written on Replacement Theology. He explains the issue:

Replacement Theology rests chiefly on the idea that the whole or part of the Abrahamic Covenant has been abolished, for it is this Covenant that promises to Israel eternal ownership of the land of Canaan.[1]

Genesis 17:7-8 clearly states the Covenant will exist forever: *I will establish my covenant between me and you [Abraham] and your offspring after you throughout their generations for an everlasting covenant, to be God to you and to your offspring after you. And I will give to you and to your offspring after you the land of your sojournings, all the land of Canaan, for an everlasting possession, and I will be their God.*

If we eradicate God's promise – as those who believe in Replacement Theology and Restorationism do – the present-day reinstatement of Israel means nothing and her only hope is in the Church.

Salvation in Christ Alone

Let me clarify that I believe salvation for both Jews and Gentiles is found exclusively in Christ Jesus (Romans 1:16-17). However,

I also believe that God's promise to grant the land of Canaan to Israel, as stated in the Abrahamic Covenant, remains intact. Israel's modern restoration to the land fulfils that promise and signifies a milestone on her journey back to her Messiah (See Ezekiel 36:24-28).

Hedding highlights the divide within the Replacement Theology camp concerning two views of the Abrahamic Covenant and exposes both as unbiblical. He then discusses how God is working out His purposes for the whole world through Israel and the Jewish people.

Israel serves as God's megaphone to communicate with the nations of the world, revealing their need for redemption. Israel has given birth to all of God's covenants, and now, through the Abrahamic Covenant, she has returned to her ancient homeland.

The ongoing conflict over Israel arises from God's unfolding plan, and Hedding urges us to support it. The church should aid Israel and her people in preparing for the arrival of her great and most blessed King (Isaiah 62:10). We should remove obstacles from Zion, yet, as he notes:

instead, we are joining in with the world, not to mention the devil, in attacking her.[2]

He continues:

Replacement theology is thus an instrument of the powers of darkness to frustrate the purpose of God, by disconnecting the Church from this final great redemptive initiative in history.[3]

He states that the church should reject this lie, return to, and rely on the promises of God concerning Israel and the Church.

Roots and Branches

You can easily discover the flaws in Replacement Theology. The idea that the Church has replaced Israel is obviously untrue when you meditate on the verses in Romans 11.

This chapter talks about how we, the Gentile believers, are a wild olive branch grafted into the natural olive tree:

some of the branches have been broken off, and you, though a wild olive shoot, have been grafted in among the others and now share in the nourishing sap from the olive root. (11.17).

This happened because of the Jews' unbelief, their blindness – they didn't accept Jesus – but we are not to boast, be arrogant or feel superior because of God's acceptance of us (v. 18 - 19). We must consider God's kindness in grafting us in – giving us salvation along with his special people – but we must also consider his sternness otherwise we too could be *"cut off"* (v.22). We must also be aware that the *"blindness"* of the Jewish people – caused by God hardening their hearts – is only temporary. When a certain number of Gentiles have become believers then God will remove the blindfold and all of God's people – Israel – will become believers (v. 26).

What is the main thing that God is telling us in this passage? Surely it is that we are grafted into His people – and we should be glad about that – but more importantly, we should be fearfully aware that we are *grafted into* them, we don't *replace* them.

Arrogance and superiority were the attitudes New Churches exhibited with their embrace of Replacement Theology, a relative success in church planting and a self-assurance that their theology was free from error.

We rejoice in our salvation which comes from faith in Christ alone and not from any benevolent attitude or acts of goodwill toward Jewish people and certainly not by observance of Jewish customs, feasts, or laws. Nevertheless, we need to remember that God's promises to his ancient people still stand, and despite their faithless wanderings, he will fulfil them.

Spiritualisation and Antisemitism

In his eye-opening study of Replacement Theology, Dr David R. Reagan outlines his journey from a blind acceptance of it to a more accurate interpretation of the Old Testament.[4] He talks about how the OT is side-lined and downgraded as God's Word. Replacement Theology teaching, whether specifically verbalised or not, spreads the idea that the OT does not mean what it says, and that you must, therefore, spiritualise it.[5]

After studying Bible prophecy more deeply, he realised

church leaders were twisting scriptures to fit man-made ideas. He asserts that this has led believers to doubt the Genesis account of creation and God's prophetic promises for the future. I have seen in my own local church, in the younger generations significantly, an abandoning of basic beliefs in God's Word. He urges us to properly interpret the Word to find its plain sense meaning and so avoid the invention of misleading doctrines like Replacement Theology.

He locates the root of the problem in Satan's hatred of the Jewish people. He explains that Satan hates the Jews with a passion for many reasons not least because God chose them to be His witness to the world, gave the world the Bible and gave us the Messiah through them.

He goes on to outline a new type of antisemitism that has spread since the horrors of Holocaust faded. He calls it anti-Zionism:

Anti-Zionism is just anti-Semitism in new, sophisticated clothes. Whereas anti-Semitism sought to drive out the Jews from the lands where they lived, anti-Zionism refuses to accept their right to live in their own land.[6]

Reading this brought me right back to where I had started: what I witnessed first-hand in Israel in that horrible detainee camp. And it reminded me how the situation is being misrepresented in the West by a biased media and blinkered church leaders.

Many Christians are now anti-Zionist, and this position is no less anti-Semitic than the secular one. Writer Michael Fryer, in his book on antisemitism, says:

rather than demonise the Jew, as Christendom did prior to the Holocaust, the Christian anti-Semite now demonises Israel, the State.[7]

This is one of the ways in which Replacement Theology is perpetuated in the churches.

A History of Hate

The studies by Dr Reagan as well as work by others such as Fryer are useful in uncovering how this heretical doctrine is rooted in the early years of Christianity's history.

Along with many other scholars, Fryer gives us insight into this:

This theology was founded by the early church fathers Eusebius, Augustine, Jerome and others who spoke against the Jewish people and their traditions, on occasion calling them swine and demons.[8]

The teaching that the church had now replaced Israel began then as a distancing from all things Jewish and from the Jewish festivals.

The early church led the persecution of Jews and the idea that the church is the spiritual Israel became lodged in our theology, despite Paul's clear teaching in the book of Romans to the contrary.

Constantine the Great, Emperor of Rome from 306 to 337 AD, initiated a persecution of the Jews which was continued more forcibly by his sons from 339 onward. He convened the Council of Nicaea in 325, which officially separated the Church from the Hebrew calendar. An example of this is how Passover was replaced with a holiday connected to pagan roots (which we now celebrate as Easter).

The Council made all the decisions and only later wrote a letter to the churches summarising what they had done. In it, Constantine encouraged the separation claiming that Jews were responsible for killing Jesus and that the churches should have nothing to do with them.

From then on Jews would steadily become second-class citizens of the (Roman) Empire.[9]

Romans 11 encourages us to remember our Hebraic roots (v. 18). There are many commentators on this subject who talk in various ways about an inadequate and incomplete view of scripture and of God that has developed in the church because we have tended to read the Bible from a Hellenised point of view rather than a Hebraic one.

Dwight Pryor, in his book *A Different God*, raises the point that we Christians may be worshipping a different God to the one that the Bible presents because he is, and wants to be known as, the God of Israel, the God of Abraham, Isaac and Jacob.

Pryor highlights something I, too, have noticed about the preaching in churches today. It seems that, when formulating the Church's essential theology, much of the Hebrew Bible, except perhaps the first three chapters of Genesis, is not regarded as pertinent. He continues:

Everything else is for illustrations, for inspiration, and perhaps for spiritual edification, but has nothing decisive to say about God's story in the earth.[10]

Pryor shows us how, when it comes to telling God's Big Story, we Christians can do it without any reference whatsoever to the God of Israel! We can talk about creation, skip on to how God, displeased by man's rebellion, sent a Redeemer to display his love (rather than His judgement). We then proclaim that all who call upon the Redeemer are saved and receive a place in the world to come. End of story.

Pryor urges us to reassess this narrative because, in reading Genesis, we find three chapters allocated to Creation and the Fall, but thirty-eight chapters allocated to the story of Abraham and his family. He points out that:

from the Hebraic point of view Genesis 1-11 is the prelude to the main story.[11]

The Scandal of Particularity
The role of postmodernism is relevant to this discussion. In researching Abraham's call, I encountered what some call "The Scandal of Particularity." This questions why Israel was chosen to carry the promise, a concept that can be unsettling to postmodern sensibilities. The notion of a "chosen race" is troubling to many, including some within the church. Those who oppose this idea often do so because they reject God's methods and, by doing this, can start to reject God himself. They seek a democratic "level playing field" and the concept of a human-constructed, elusive "fair society."

C.S. Lewis outlines a secular view that many in the church now prefer, arguing that all nations and individuals should start on equal footing in their search for God, or even that all religions are equally true. However, he strongly asserts that:

...Christianity makes no concessions to this point of view.[12]

Lewis goes on to describe the highly selective and undemocratic process of choosing Abraham: we read in Genesis how the knowledge of God had been universally lost or obscured, and yet God picks out one man from the whole earth, separates him from his usual surroundings and sends him into a strange country, all so that he would be:

...the ancestor of a nation who are to carry the knowledge of the true God.[13]

In response to those who find this concept scandalous, I would simply say we need to understand that God's ways are not our ways.

A Summary of this Chapter

Many groups within the church, possibly due to a lack of understanding on the part of their leaders, have been blind to the truths discussed in this section. This blindness affects younger generations, new converts, those new to this country, and some others who have varying degrees of biblical knowledge due to spiritual immaturity or age. We observed how scriptures have been taken out of context or spiritualised to fit a Replacement Theology view that ignores God's Covenants.

We saw how Church history reveals a drift away from our Hebraic roots as a particular type of Christianity – one that held to Replacement Theology – became an established part of the religious landscape, and how, as a tool of the Powers of Darkness, it seriously hinders God's purposes.

We saw how the 'Scandal of Particularity' revealed strong connections to our contemporary postmodern views about not being seen to be exclusive.

It would help our understanding of these things if the spiritualisation of the prophetic and other scriptures were discarded in favour of a plain sense reading.

We also identified the satanic roots of the hatred aimed at Israel. The existence of Israel is a sign of the inevitable fulfilment of God's covenant purposes for her so she will always be at the centre of a global battle for truth. She is also a sign of the soon return of Messiah. Jesus was born in Israel, died in Israel, rose again in Israel and, when he returns, it will be to Israel.

In an assessment of why all this hatred is aimed at the Jews I came to a logical conclusion. You don't have to be a theologian to know that the enemy is very clever, and he is not going to waste his time attacking the Jews if they are no longer part of God's plan. He is not going to waste his time inciting violence toward Israel if that land and its people have no biblical significance and no part in the plan of God.

I studied the scriptures relating to Replacement Theology and Anti-Semitism and the history of these subjects, to discover the origins of these lies. I did this and you can too, and I have provided a list of resources in the Appendix for those seeking truth.

If you study Replacement Theology and its effects on the church in the West then it is almost impossible to avoid coming across its strong connection to Restorationism, a.k.a. Kingdom Now beliefs. I discuss this in the next chapter.

Notes:

[1] Hedding, M. *The Challenge of Replacement Theology* at:
https://www.icej.org/understand-israel/biblical-teachings/the-challenge-of-replacement-theology/

[2] Ibid

[3] Ibid

[4] *The Evil of Replacement Theology* (Dr David Reagan, Lion and Lamb Ministries) at:
http://christinprophecy.org/articles/the-evil-of-replacement-theology/

[5] Spiritualisation. Drawing conclusions at the price of proper interpretation and making the Bible say what you want it to say leads to serious error. Spiritualisation adds meanings to Bible passages that are not there and is a mishandling of God's word.

[6] Ibid

[7] Fryer, M. *Anti-Zionism, the New Anti-Semitism*, Father's House Publications, Queensferry, p10.

[8] Ibid, p74

[9] *Jewish Currents* (2018), *Emperor Constantine and the Jews* at:
https://jewishcurrents.org/emperor-constantine-and-the-jews/

[10] Pryor, D. A. (2007), *A Different God? Reassessing the Place of Israel and the Church in God's Story*, Center for Judaic-Christian Studies, Dayton Ohio, p9

[11] Ibid, p9

[12] Lewis, C. S. (1947), *Miracles*, London, Harper Collins, as quoted in Floyd, R. (2009), *Why Mary?* C. S. Lewis on the Scandal of Particularity, at: https://richardlfloyd.com/2009/12/17/

[13] Ibid, p173

Chapter 10

DRAGGING THE KINGDOM TO EARTH

Restorationism or Kingdom Now Ideology

Restorationism had to be coupled with Replacement Theology. If the truth about God's plan for the world, including Israel's part in this, and Jesus's 1000-year reign, is rejected, the vacuum must be filled with something else. Restorationism created unmet expectations, leaving many Christians disillusioned. But few in the churches or New Churches today have heard of Restorationism, so does it matter?

It matters not only because of its historical significance but also due to its potential influence today.

In Chapter three, in *A Fork in the Road*, I shared my personal experience of this misguided teaching. It took root in the consciousness of the church, particularly the New Churches, causing a significant derailment. This teaching, fundamental to New Churches, can be traced back its origins in The Latter Rain movement.

Some in New Church streams may claim they are no longer influenced by it, and the term itself may rarely be mentioned, but its core ideas persist. The label is less important than the beliefs and practices it represents. These concepts can undermine faith and erode trust in the Lord.

To explain, let's dive into what Restorationism is and how its teachings still resonate in the church.

Restorationism – an Alternative Kingdom

So, what are these beliefs? To understand them we need to go back to the 1940s. Back to the early influences of the New

Churches found in a man called Franklin Hall who prophesied what he said would be:

... the dawn of a new period of prophetic revelation which would result in a worldwide spiritual revival brought about through prayer and fasting. He foretold a reign of righteousness and great power which would bring forth a Joel's army to conquer the nations. But he also said that prayer with fasting to any god is effective! William Branham then came to the fore prophesying a great end-time revival, with a second Pentecost Latter Rain church which God was calling out from the denominations to conquer the world.[1]

William Branham's teaching influenced churches in North Battleford, Canada, which promoted the notion that God was raising up apostles and prophets to form and lead a new, glorious church. This church would be the true Israel of God in the new age now being established. It was also taught that:

the wicked would be removed from the earth and that, having defeated the heavenly powers, the elite would remain to reign on earth.[2]

When I discovered this root, I saw how it aligned with the teaching I had heard at the Bible weeks from the 1970s through to the 1990s.

I also remembered hearing one of the leaders of my New Church stream, speaking in the mid 2000s, refer to this when teaching from some passages in Isaiah:

Though you search for your enemies, you will not find them. Those that war against you will be as nothing at all.
(Isaiah 41:22).

He pointed at one or two people in the congregation, as preachers often do, and commented to them and the rest of us how we will be so happy when the evil people are taken out of the way. He never explained what he meant by this – and no one asked him.

In 1970s Britain, the New Churches, then known as the House Church movement, exemplified the Restorationism or Kingdom Now paradigm which modelled the idea that:

... the church will do most of the work of the Kingdom before the second coming of Christ. The church will conquer the nations, controlling all its major institutions and the 'sons of God' will be manifested and take the land for Jesus.[3]

The basic concept of Restorationism was born out of a series of misinterpretations of various scriptures. One was a wrong understanding of Acts 3.21 where it says,

For he must remain in heaven until the time for the final restoration of all things ... (21a, NLT)

which was taught to mean that God will restore the Church to a powerful, honoured and praised global institution before Jesus returns. But the false teaching fails to articulate what the rest of the verse says. It says quite clearly that this restoration is that which God promised to do through the fulfilment of Old Testament prophecies. Nowhere in the Old Testament is the restoration of all things foreseen by any of the Hebrew prophets before the return of the Messiah.

The Latter Rain teachings were further promoted by the American minister, William Branham. He continued in a similar vein by prophesying a great end-time revival through the movement. Proponents of Latter Rain teachings such as Branham, Ern Baxter, and Jack Coe, in attempting to address a dryness they perceived in Evangelicalism and Pentecostalism, made a series of doctrinal and practical changes. These changes separated the movement from its traditional Pentecostal background.

Despite this, the teachings quickly spread throughout the United States and around the world, influencing many within Pentecostalism. Much of this teaching was absorbed into the charismatic movement of the UK.

Many Christian commentators recognise Branham as the: *"principal architect of Restorationist thought"* for Charismatics. [4]

Latter Rain teaching was rejected by large groups of classical Pentecostals and in 1949 the General Council of the Assemblies of God USA declared their extreme teachings and practices as unfounded scripturally and declared their disapproval of the so-called New Order of the Latter Rain.

One of the practices they dismissed was the custom of the laying on of hands to transfer power and various gifts and ministries.

Despite this, the influence of the Latter Rain movement spread to the UK churches. Paul Cain, one of the new types of 'prophets' and a key leader in the movement, had a prominent role in the early days of New Frontiers, a new house church group formed in the UK. Cain had been a disciple of William Branham and had never renounced Branham's heretical teachings that caused him to be ejected from the Pentecostal movement. Cain taught that God would raise-up a 'new breed' of Christians who would move in healing power and supernatural signs and wonders. They would be immortal.

He prophesied over the leaders of New Frontiers that the organisation would introduce a new kind of Christianity to the world. I clearly remember the strapline *"Changing the expression of Christianity around the world"* that New Frontiers adopted and used as their mission statement.

Other key Latter Rain people, besides Branham and Cain, were Bill Hamon, James Goll, John Paul Jackson and Mike Bickle. They were advocates of the teaching in America while several church leaders such as Gerald Coates, Colin Urquhart and Terry Virgo began to promote it in the UK.

A newly emerging group based in the Kansas City Fellowship, a church in Missouri, US, became known as the "Kansas City Prophets" because of their emphasis on prophecy. It could be argued that they were the founders of the Apostolic-Prophetic Movement. This would later become known in some circles as the New Apostolic Reformation, the (NAR), although many involved in this are unaware of this name.

Some of these 'prophets' were exposed for involvement in gross sexual sin, obvious false teaching, and unfulfilled prophecy. Their prophecies, not localised or personal, were powerfully directive in terms of leading the church into future error on a global scale.

In Chapter three, I mentioned John Wimber, a former rock band leader who rose to prominence during that period. He was used by the Kansas City Fellowship to bring these damaging heresies into the UK. Paul Cain prophesied that a great revival would begin in the UK in 1990 and Wimber was to come over and lead it. Meetings at Holy Trinity Brompton and the Excel Centre, East London, went ahead despite objections from some church leaders, because others had issued a statement lending their support to the Kansas City Fellowship team and urging people to attend.

There was no revival.

Wimber went back to the US completely dispirited. Shortly after this he was diagnosed with cancer of the throat. He excluded Paul Cain and Bob Jones from his ministry team and expelled Kansas City Fellowship from the Vineyard group of churches of which he was a founder member.

Much of the history concerning the foundations of the New Churches, New Frontiers, and the Latter Rain movement has been extensively documented, so I will not delve into it further. I encourage you to conduct your own research, use the references provided, and seek additional sources. Seek God, pray, and study your Bible in relation to these matters.

The Bible verses used to support Restorationism have been taken out of context, resulting in a very unreliable foundation for an individual's Christian life, the life of a local church, and the structure of any church stream or organisation. It is akin to building on a sandbank.

A Return to Common Sense

Once my eyes were opened, I realised these ideas were self-deluding fantasies, leading the church astray. I revisited the teachings from Bible Weeks and church sermons, steeped in prayer. I reexamined prophetic verses, searching for their plain meanings.

In Chapter 3, I wrote about Isaiah 60:1-5 (*Arise, shine; for your light has come* ... etc.) but I didn't know then how these verses were twisted to promote false notions.

In the same chapter, in the section, *A Fork in the Road*, I told of my initial belief and enthusiasm for these ideas, but a closer look later unveiled glaring flaws.

Other sections of scripture were twisted to say the church would gain importance and influence in the world drawing many people in through national and global revival.

The verses from Isaiah 2 about *"the mountain of the Lord"* also quoted in Chapter 3 were misinterpreted to say similar things. Teaching on the quote will usually start at verse 2 while verse 1, showing the context to be a prophecy concerning Judah and Jerusalem, gets left out. It must be quite tricky for preachers who believe in Replacement Theology to ensure they edit out the many references to Israel, the Jewish people, Zion, Jerusalem and similar things. Verse 4 of this passage says that the people of the nations of the world will beat their swords into ploughshares, their swords into pruning hooks and study war no more.

Is that really going to happen now, within this church age?

The Isaiah 58:12 prophecy, about restoring ancient ruins, quoted in the same section, was also taken out of context. It was used recklessly to suggest the church would rebuild a damaged society but is actually about something that happens after Israel's regathering and repentance.

The well-known prophecy about the valley of dry bones in Ezekiel 37 is not about the restoration of the church, as we heard, but about the return of scattered Jews to their promised land.

Similarly, Isaiah 54:2, about enlarging one's tent, was often used as a prompt to encourage increases in congregation size and new church plantings. The proper context is that of God having to discipline the nation of Israel because of their sin but then having compassion on them and settling them in their own land. This is something that God does following their chastisement.

The reason I have heard Isaiah 54:2 quoted so often in New

Frontiers circles is, I believe, because it is part of the prophecy that Paul Cain gave to leaders at the founding of New Frontiers. One could argue that it is not unreasonable to use the wording of these prophecies in a general sense to give encouragement to contemporary believers but because they were used in close alignment with Restorationist aims it became misleading. The call to *"enlarge the place of your tent"* was never about stirring up church growth – the Church did not exist then!

Similarly, the verses from the book of Joel, mentioned in Chapter 9, were used wrongly to persuade the churches they will become a mighty army. It was taught that God was going to make the church a powerful force in the world that would influence every part of society: the church would *"leap over mountaintops, scale walls"*, and *"rush upon the cities"*. The truth is that the army described here is a terrible judgement sent by God on the nation because of their sin (parts conveniently left out) and is followed by a heartfelt call to repent so that this retribution might be avoided.

The passage from Isaiah 43 frequently quoted to encourage congregations to embrace questionable manifestations emanating from the Toronto Blessing and the Prophetic Movement was also taken out of context. This teaching required believers to embrace these things often without testing them. In truth, these scriptures, I first mentioned in Chapter 4, describe God's faithfulness in bringing Israel back to their homeland. God reminds them of his faithfulness and compares it with their faithlessness but assures them that, despite this, he will bring them home and settle them. *That* is the *"new thing"*.

All these teachings, using isolated verses to support distorted ideas, omitted the negative aspects of God's judgment due to idolatry, pride, and spiritual adultery. No clear explanation was offered. The impression given was that these negative-sounding verses related to an Old Testament God who is "not like that now."

Because the Old Testament scriptures were considered less important than the New, these negative aspects were conveniently overlooked. As a new Christian, I accepted this teaching without questioning the muddled thinking. Many other verses were used to promote false doctrines, forming the shaky foundations of many of the New Church streams.

God still desires to do wonderful things through the church but not before repentance. If God grants us repentance, any marvels that follow should not be seen as the fulfillment of Restorationist or Kingdom Now policies but because of God's grace. New Church plantings and evangelism have seen success, but greater success could have been achieved if the church had listened to God. Most of the success in New Church growth has been achieved despite these policies not because of them.

Repentance is necessary for years of false teaching, incomplete presentation of God's word, wrong attitudes toward Israel, and not presenting God's word in the public sphere. Revival remains a possibility, but time is running out.

The Centre Cannot Hold

On the 14th of August 2018 the Polcevera Bridge in Genoa, Italy, collapsed killing 43 people and injuring 13. The bridge was an impressive landmark in the city. Thought of as one of the most famous road bridges in Italy, it appeared to be an outstanding work of design and engineering.

When the bridge failed, 17 cars and 10 lorries fell some 50 metres as a section of the bridge 260 metres long carrying four lanes of traffic plunged into the valley below.

Two enquiries, one into the structural details of the bridge and one as a criminal investigation, studied all the evidence and concluded that the disaster was predictable and could have been avoided.

The designer, Ricardo Morandi, had pioneered a new way of building bridges by embedding steel cables in concrete with the aim of creating longer spans. Three huge trusses 90 metres high supported the road with these cables. In attempting to prevent rusting, the cables were covered in concrete but one of the cables inside the concrete shell snapped. CCTV footage showed that once one of the cables snapped it caused a fatal loss of the tension vital to maintain the bridge's construction. This put tremendous pressure on other parts, unbalancing the whole structure, which led to a complete collapse. The investigations revealed that the steel cables inside the concrete had become corroded. Because the cables were hidden by the concrete it was impossible to be aware of the corrosion or assess how bad it was. The faults were hidden.

As I watched a TV documentary[5] about this tragedy, I couldn't help but draw parallels to an impending disaster in the church. Faults in the teachings of Western churches, particularly the New Churches, are concealed beneath an exterior of self-assurance and apparent success. The teaching is deeply embedded, making the faults difficult to detect. The teaching is part of the DNA of these churches.

I felt uneasy about the safety of the congregations in these churches. As hard times come, the churches may not stand, and believers, long promised a forthcoming revival, will become disheartened. It will be obvious to most that the Kingdom of God is not being established on the earth in the way that had been taught for years and the disillusioned will be in danger of turning away - as many have already done so. Unless corrective measures are taken, disaster looms.

I was first deceived by these ideas in the late 1970s and, despite the turmoil they've caused, they persist. Unearthing these roots and errors was disheartening but made worse by recognising the enemy's efforts to fabricate other deceptions which I will point to in a following section.

Our Journey So Far

I hope this exploration has shed light on the significance of the Jewish people and their God-given land. Israel remains a central focus in God's plan for the world in these last days. I hope you can now see that wayward Israel is still the apple of God's eye and that animosity toward Israel puts you, your church or church stream in danger. The combination of Kingdom Now and Restorationist beliefs, born out of Replacement Theology, has plagued the churches, falsely promising that Apostles and Prophets would establish God's Kingdom on earth during the Church Age.

For over 40 years, proponents of this false teaching have made it into a tradition, largely due to the ignorance of many believers who accept it without question. You can avoid being deceived by not spiritualising Old Testament prophecies–read them at face value where appropriate. Commentaries and devotional study aids are listed in the Appendix to help you do this.

Don't be fearful but be informed and prepared. The world faces significant issues, often ignored by Western churches. A global conspiracy exists, orchestrated by the evil one. He has led the world to believe that God's creation is a cosmic accident, promoting theories contrary to the Biblical account. If he can beguile the world with these ideas, he can also beguile regarding the things I have written about so far and address in the following chapters. Understanding current issues will provide peace in troubled times if you draw close to the Lord and seek his guidance.

Shadowlands

The false teachings previously mentioned have infiltrated and weakened the Church. But I must draw attention to two additional forces operating from secular realms. We now exist in a place where these influences cast a shadow over the Church, affecting everything it does.

I will not delve into these issues here, as my intention is not to detract from the more crucial and urgent matters discussed in the main body of this book. However, you can find a detailed account of my research into these subjects in the Appendix. One topic is the New Age Movement, and the other is Cultural Marxism.

There is a perilous intersection between the Church and the New Age Movement, necessitating awareness of its influences and history. I have traced the historical roots of the New Age Movement, identified key figures like Alice Bailey, and debunked the notion that it is merely a fringe phenomenon of the past. The New Age Movement illuminates the contemporary landscape where influential academics and progressives wield global influence, subtly disseminating ideologies that threaten traditional Christian teachings.

I investigated the insidious undercurrents of Cultural Marxism and its associated philosophies, unravelling the intricate web they weave around the foundations of Western culture. I discovered dangerous ideologies that have stealthily eroded values crucial for a stable society. My exploration includes a detailed examination of the movement's origins, tracing back to influential figures, dissecting their writings, intentions, and the mechanisms through which their ideologies infiltrated and corroded societal norms.

As I investigated, a resounding wake-up call emerged–a warning that needed to be heard by church leaders and congregants who may unwittingly be caught in the currents of this "progressive" ideology. Many sceptics dismiss Cultural Marxism as a mere 'conspiracy theory,' but I found compelling evidence to counter this notion, establishing the credibility of my concerns.

Learning about its devastating ideology prompted reflections on my youth and the changes that happened during that time. I began to see the underlying causes of the rebellion and promiscuity of the 1960s and 70s. Those changes started slowly but have since gathered pace.

Cultural Marxism has permeated the very fabric of global society. Academics and progressives in influential positions propel the ideology forward, shaping societies worldwide.

There is a need to recognise this form of Marxism that is eroding Western culture. It is a pervasive force demanding a vigilant response from the Church and its members. It is the root cause and means by which Christians will face increasing persecution, making it imperative to understand it.

It is surprising how similar the aims of these two movements are which indicates that the same force is behind each of them.

See the Appendix for further reading on these two important subjects.

Notes:

[1] Various contributors, (1995), *Charismatic Crossroads*, London, PWM Team Ministries, p6

[2] Ibid, p7

[3] Ibid, p7

[4] *See: https://en.wikipedia.org/wiki/William M. Branham*

[5] BBC 2 TV, (2019), *When Bridges Collapse: The Genoa Disaster*, Broadcast 12th August 2021.

Chapter 11

SUBVERTING THE CHURCH

The Plot Thickens.

I have just mentioned two oppressive movements now operating in society that have one aim: to supress, persecute and eliminate the Church, and Israel and the Jews.

The next issues are more church related than societal.

To begin an examination of these things I must refer you back to past experiences of church life and teaching. My investigations and studies of Replacement Theology and Restorationism showed them to be false teachings. I have had to renounce them before God and repent of my involvement.

You may be wondering whatever could be next. I will tell you what I found.

Highjacked

I believe that the move of God, called the Renewal Movement, that swept through the UK in the 1970s was a genuine move of God. He showed the church his power was available to sincere and authentic believers so that others would be brought into the Kingdom of God. But sadly, this movement got hijacked by those who wanted to elevate themselves, their own ministry, their church, or church stream.

Toronto - A New Church delusion

When telling the story of my encounters with Restorationism and Kingdom Now theology, as disseminated at various Bible Weeks and in the New Churches, I used the sub-title *A Fork in the Road* for that section because it was a new road that appeared to lead to new revelations about the Kingdom of God on earth.

Later, when I encountered the Toronto Blessing and the introduction of the Apostolic and Prophetic movement into the UK with its emphasis on signs and wonders I thought this too would further increase the church's power in society. I thought it would intensify our witness to a world that was becoming increasingly godless.

Hindsight is a wonderful thing, especially when illuminated by God. I now see that these things are distractions the enemy has used and is using to divert the church from its true calling.

Who Switched the Points?

On a railway line there are many places where you can see points on the track. Points are movable sections of the railway track which allow trains to move from one line to another. But like railway signals, points can fail. If a train is wrongly moved from one track to another the passengers on that train might not notice any difference in their journey. They do not realise they are on the wrong track. Everything looks the same. Eventually, the track will veer off taking you in a different direction or you will have a head-on collision, or both. I now believe that this is what happened with what came to be known as The Toronto Blessing. Large parts of the church have been side-tracked and are no longer with God.

In previous sections I dealt with the issue of Restorationism and Kingdom Now teaching. But what about the so-called 'Blessing' that came out of Toronto? Many people claimed that they had been revitalised by it. What is the truth about this movement and its effect on individuals and churches in the UK?

Earlier in this book I gave a very personal account of my involvement, my enthusiasm for, and my dissemination of the ideas and doctrines inherent in this movement. The 'Blessing' brought great promise to the churches of the UK when it was first imported from the US not least because it stirred-up some of those hopes that had started to fade. Hopes that something great was about to happen – that revival was imminent.

There was no revival.

What we witnessed was a mixture; some believers testified to having a greater love for Jesus and commitment to the Gospel; there was talk of changed lives. I was in the thick of it. There was such a hunger to see God move and I think we all exaggerated what we experienced. Most of the testimonies were such that it was hard to prove any lasting change had taken place.

I now see that blind acceptance of the manifestations experienced in this movement proved to be wrong and encouragement to not analyse what was happening was unscriptural and dangerous.

I studied the Bible and other writings regarding the practice of laying on of hands for impartation of the 'Blessing' or associated gifts. I found this practice as it happened then, and still happens today, is not scriptural.

There are many scriptures that tell how the Apostles laid hands so that gifts would be received by others, but these were given *by God* directly to the recipient. What was happening within the Toronto movement was that ministers were claiming to be able to impart either the "Blessing" or some other gift directly *from themselves*. This often happened after the minister in question had received the 'Blessing' or other impartation from someone else in the same way.

I discovered in Haggai 2:10-14 the explanation of why this is so perilous. These verses make it clear: things that can defile you are transmitted in this way, but blessings cannot be passed on. Nevertheless, born again believers who are in a right relationship with God and who do not willingly submit to an evil spirit are protected by the shed blood of Christ. An examination of this practice will reveal that you cannot get a blessing from God in one location, take it somewhere else, and pass it on to another person. It begs the question: what was being imparted?

In my description of how signs accompanying the 'Blessing' manifested themselves I referred to the jerking and convulsing. Upon reflection I now see that this was either fleshly or, sometimes, demonic. Regarding that which became known as the 'Toronto Twitch' I can see how it was often learned behaviour or a psychological reaction but in some cases I fear it was something much worse, not least because of its involuntary nature. Other manifestations, such as uncontrollable laughter, being 'Slain in the Spirit', rolling on the floor and going into trance-like states had similar dubious causes that should have been tested but never were.

I exhibited signs of this phenomenon myself. I have had to repent and renounce involvement in them and in the movement that birthed them. I had hands laid on me many times during the height of my involvement in this movement. I never questioned if the person 'blessing' me believed it was coming from him, from God, or elsewhere. When God showed me the error of my ways I repented and renounced it all.

Dear believer, if you have ever had 'impartations' of any kind or displayed any of these manifestations or behaviours then I plead with you to renounce your involvement before God, ask his forgiveness and repent of them as soon as you can.

Occult Roots

While researching the Toronto Blessing, I found that its manifestations had parallels with questionable roots. When a visiting speaker or church leader laid hands on someone to impart a 'blessing,' it often resulted in them falling over as a sign of surrender, influenced by peer pressure at times.

Some commentators have compared this to the Hindu Shakti-pat experience of 'Kundalini Awakening.' One researcher found how the idea was picked up by William Branham (remember him?) on a trip to India, likely introducing it to the US in the early days of the Latter Rain movement. The best way to describe the experiences mimicked by the Toronto Blessing is to refer to those actively engaged in them. Many websites validate and encourage these practices. This extract comes from one of them:

Shaktipat can be given by a kundalini guru or an enlightened spiritual master in the form of a mantra (sacred words) or by

*a look or glance, a touch, usually on the ajna chakra, (third
eye, the forehead), by thought, by an object like a piece of fruit
or a flower, and even by telephone, fax, or these days over the
internet.*[1]

This reminded me of the many meetings I'd been in where
preachers would line up members of the congregation to
receive an impartation. They often touched the recipient,
sometimes with just one finger, in the middle of the forehead.
And I remembered copying this myself a few times when praying
for others. I saw this happen when I was there in person but also
in videos and TV programmes of "revivals" in other parts of the
world, Pensacola and Lakeland for example. Online videos of
people experiencing Shaktipat and Kundalini Awakening show
striking similarities to behaviours in Christian gatherings where
the 'Blessing' was imparted.

There are many books, articles and documents that analyse
the phenomenon of the Toronto Blessing but a key piece
of work I found is the 302-page Doctorate Thesis by South
African, Stephanus Pretorius. Written in 2002, it is an in-depth
study that many researchers of this topic like me have used
and referred to. The author explores many disciplines to make
sense of what went on in Toronto in the mid-1990s. He comes
at the subject from every angle that any enquirer could possibly
be concerned with and, further to this, locates it in the context
of other 'moves of God' and wider expressions of Christian
spirituality.

He evaluates how the Toronto Blessing corresponds to
spirituality in general and Christian spirituality in particular.
He examines the manifestations occurring at Toronto Blessing
events with respect to the Bible and compares them to the Hindu
experience of 'Kundalini awakening'. He then investigates the
role of neuroscience, specific psychological processes (e.g.,
hypnosis, mass hysteria), and the ways our bodies and minds
experience and interpret spiritual phenomena.

From the introduction to Pretorius's Study:

Although Charismatics claim that the Toronto Blessing has a sound biblical foundation, no evidence to support this claim has been found. However, striking similarities are found between the manifestations of the Toronto Blessing and the techniques used in the 'Kundalini awakening' for the transference of energy. Finally, the major findings of this study support the conclusion that the Toronto Blessing is largely the result of psychological techniques. The possibility of Godly intervention is not totally excluded, but caution is urged, so as to be aware of extraneous factors that create similar manifestations. While it is agreed that the Toronto Blessing can be seen as an expression of spirituality in a broad sense, nevertheless, it cannot be viewed as an expression of Christian spirituality in the Charismatic Movement.[2]

Another study by The Centre for Contemporary Ministry, produced a report published in 1995 which corroborates these findings, noting genuine blessings, fleshly activity, and even demonic counterfeiting in the Toronto Blessing. The report, entitled *Charismatic Crossroads*[3] came out of a conference called after grave concerns were raised.

Published in booklet form the Crossroads report is nowhere near as long as the Pretorius thesis, comprising only 20 pages, but nevertheless constitutes a thorough examination that comes to the same conclusions: some genuine blessing, some fleshly activity and notably, some demonic counterfeiting of Christian spirituality.

The participation of church members in signs and wonders movements, as I experienced in my local church, varied in impact. Church leaders displayed manifestations, often to align with trends, but there was a lack of biblical scrutiny.

I now wonder how I got taken in by all this and must conclude that I did not pause to judge these events. All the manifestations mentioned above and sometimes things much worse such as the spiritual drunkenness, the 'fire tunnels' and the clairvoyance posing as 'words of knowledge' should have been exposed by the leaders for what it was.

One of the most nefarious of these aberrations was the

ministry of the visiting speaker Trevor Baker I referred to earlier. I now see that presenting the Holy Spirit to the congregation as an orb or ball that could be kicked in any direction – which he demonstrated – was a terrible offence against the Lord. If it was not absolute blasphemy, then it was not far short of it! I am now dumbfounded as to how the leaders of my church and church stream consented to such teaching. Correction should have been brought to him and to the church but there was a total lack of discernment.

Considering my investigations into the history of 'Toronto' with its origins in the Latter Rain movement it was not difficult for me to see how earlier drifting away from the truth had prepared the ground for these errors to take root in the church. As the Pretorius Study indicates:

Teachings with underlying metaphysical principles emphasizing the importance of supernatural manifestations, without discerning that 'supernatural' manifestations could also be brought on by human intervention as well as demonic influence, created a platform for and an easy acceptance amongst their members of 'strange' manifestations as interventions of God.[4]

For newcomers to the church or younger believers, I encourage you to consider these foundational belief systems. While I challenge you to think about these issues, do not fear. If you are a true believer, you are safe, regardless of your awareness or lack of it so, do not worry. Keep going back to God with any concerns you may have.

A Summary of This Chapter

The Renewal Movement in the 1970s was God-given but derailed by false teachings like Restorationism and Kingdom Now theology. Succumbing to these lies made us vulnerable to further deception, such as the mixed blessings from Toronto.

One of the sins that led to judgement coming on Israel such as their ensuing captivity was the lack of discernment which should have been shown by the leaders. God pointed this out through Ezekiel:

Her priests do violence to my law and profane my holy things; they do not distinguish between the holy and the common; they teach that there is no difference between the unclean and the clean ... Ezekiel 22: 26a.

The enemy is not content with that level of devastation in the church and is now busy morphing it all into something even worse. This emerging monster is the signs and wonders movement that I was so heavily involved in. It originated in the US but has spread all over the world. It has also been called the prophetic movement or the apostolic and prophetic movement but is now better known as the NAR.

Notes:

[1] See: https://aadinathkundaliniyogafoundation.org

[2] http://uir.unisa.ac.za/handle/10500/15821 last accessed 05.09.18

[3] Various contributors, (1995), *Charismatic Crossroads*, London, PWM Team Ministries.

[4] Ibid, p226.

Chapter 12

THE NAR

All That Glistens

The New Apostolic Reformation (NAR) represents the same teachings mentioned earlier in this book: the Latter Rain Movement of the 1940s, Kingdom Now and Restorationist beliefs, the Kansas City Prophets, the Toronto Blessing, and its offshoots, including the Brownsville/Pensacola and Lakeland Florida 'revivals'.

When I began compiling this publication, I had numerous books by NAR proponents on my shelf: Bill Johnson (5 books), Heidi Baker (2), Carole Arnott (1), Chris Valleton (1), and 13 others by NAR authors. Discovering the serious errors in them prompted my desire to discard them which I quickly did. Some of these books wouldn't seem out of place in a New Age Bookshop. Besides books, NAR ideology is also spread through music, particularly targeting young people.

Another New Church Delusion

Initially, I was apprehensive upon realising the errors in these movements and my deep involvement in them. Over time, as God brought things back to my memory, I was able to renounce and repent. Reflecting on the beliefs I once embraced, such as false signs and wonders, manna, gold fillings, and gemstones, I'm amazed at my naivety. Events like the Patricia King Conference in Torquay, where I hoped to witness these phenomena, I now avoid.

One of the most alarming is the gold dust phenomenon. Whether it appears on objects, people, or in clouds, it is said to be a sign of the glory of God. In the PhD Thesis, referred to earlier, Stephanus Pretorius suggests further study:

It would be an interesting study to investigate the 'gold filling' and 'golden dust' phenomenon that is also viewed as a supernatural manifestation of God...[1]

I did some investigation myself. There are no references to such things in the Bible or general church history, but I did find references in research by Albert James Dager, a writer, editor, publisher, and apologist. In his paper, *Kingdom Theology Defined*, he traces these ideas to the teachings of Franklin Hall, who we met earlier.

In a subsection titled *Occult Influences*, Dager quotes Hall's claims about an "Immortal Substance" that comes upon the believer as a fine gold and silver sparkling material, potentially from an unidentified flying object (UFO).

In Hall's words, *"The sparkling shining FINE GOLD and SILVER are seen upon their SKIN, brought about through the faith-power of impartation.*[2]

Hall also asserts that the Zodiac is a representation of the Gospel and that he had attained a degree of "Immortality" affecting everything he encountered. His writings include strange statements, often hard to understand, such as claims that some believers will be clothed with the "Immortality," the supernatural, sparkling substance, making it easy for them to fly up into the Glory Cloud.

A further paper by Shawn Nelson outlines problems when examining NAR characteristics, practices, and beliefs. In a section titled *Evidence of Supernatural Activity Being Faked*, he describes some concerning trends:

There is good evidence that these so-called manifestations are simply fake. A veteran professional jeweller and gemmologist of forty-four years was given three samples of gold dust from three different "glory cloud" events. When examined under his jeweller's double microscope, two samples were found to be mylar (synthetic man-made plastic) and one was mica (fool's gold). In short, "none has been gold."[3]

The jeweller also tested samples of "gemstones" from "angels" appearing in church services, which were found to be "synthetic, man-made stones."

A geochemist from the University of Toronto investigated the "gold dust" and found it did not contain any gold or platinum but was a type of plastic film. A U.S. Geological Survey study reached the same conclusions.

Further to this Nelson cites evidence of people, some of them pastors, admitting to planting gemstones to 'seed' people's faith in the supernatural. He tells of people being caught planting fake jewels on the floors of churches and putting gold glitter on themselves and claiming that God was blessing them with special favour. Nelson questions where the fear of God is when Christians would fabricate a miracle?

YouTube features a widely viewed 'Glory Cloud' video from Bethel Church in Redding, California, generating controversy. As believers, it's essential to question these occurrences, because they may become more prevalent in these last days.

I am not someone coming to this subject as an outsider having made it clear, I was very much involved in the movement, more than most in my local church, but I now see the error in it. Because of this I ask you to be alert and test everything. I challenge you to find and watch this 'Glory Cloud' video and others like it. Try to come to a firm decision about what you think.

I challenge you to seek God, pray and study the Word with emphases on characters in the Bible who have encountered the glory of God. What were their reactions?[4] If, after doing that, you believe that this event is 'of God' then I can only commend you for looking into it as best you can. If you conclude that it is not 'of God' or suspect in any way then you have only two options left regarding your assessment: either it is a man-made occurrence (which then must involve knowledge, whether partial or complete, by the organisers or hosts of the event) or it is demonic. I am sorry if you think this is blunt, but this is very serious, and we need to see things as they are. We need to know

God, his Word, his ways, and his voice.

I know several people who, having initially been enchanted by the music originating from NAR organisations, have presumed that the ministry and teaching from them must be reliable. They have then joined the organisation or attended Schools of Supernatural Ministry sometimes leaving home for a year or more only to return and face times of deep disappointment because the promises of an exciting life of spiritual power and miracles never come to fruition.

The music is the hook that catches people, and the songs are now sung in many churches globally. I am not saying that the lyrics of all these choruses are unbiblical – although a few have been called in to question – but that when used in church gatherings they make a statement to the believers. The leaders of the churches are allowing songs that come from unreliable sources to be used and are thereby endorsing those ministries.

They partner with them by inviting their teachers to speak at various events which declares a public approval and support for them.

As with all false teaching there is a lot of truth mixed in. (For a critique of the teaching by Bill Johnson / Bethel Church see the paper produced by the Christian Research Institute.)[5]

A Closer Look

An article written by Dr Frances Rabbitts gives a perceptive account of the history, beliefs, and culture of the NAR. In her opening paragraphs, she points out how teachings once on the fringes became mainstream in the charismatic world during the 2000s and 2010s. She shows how the NAR today encompasses a loose collection of charismatic ministries, leaders, and teachings, defying traditional denominational categories. It lacks a central organising body or a formal statement of beliefs. Many within this movement don't even recognise the term 'NAR,' although it was coined by one of its core founders, C. Peter Wagner. Some refer to it as 'network Christianity' due to its nebulous, relational nature.

Today, NAR powerhouses include Bill and Beni Johnson's Bethel Church in Redding, California (formerly AOG, now independent), Hillsong Church in Australia (also formerly AOG, now independent), Catch the Fire in Toronto (formerly Toronto Airport Vineyard, now independent), Heidi Baker's Iris Ministries and Rick Joyner's Morningstar Ministries, amongst many others. You will find songs, teachings, books and events connected with these and other NAR ministries being promoted in most charismatic churches in Britain, at inter-denominational conferences, in Christian bookshops and on Christian TV and radio.[6]

Dr Rabbitts explains how the NAR utilises social media, training programmes, and collaborations with respected ministries for networking. Since there's no official organisation behind it, she questions its spiritual driving force:

In many ways, the NAR borrows from biblical Christianity and most within the movement would still accept the basic tenets of the Gospel. It is evangelistic and charismatic; it believes the Bible is the inerrant Word of God. It also usually takes a conservative stance on moral issues, values prophecy, promotes social action and can encourage support for Israel. However, there are important aspects of the NAR which are inescapably unbiblical, which pollute and redirect genuinely-felt love for God. Indeed, while we are not disputing the sincerity of ordinary believers caught up in the NAR movement, we believe that, followed thoroughly and consistently, it promotes 'a different Jesus, a different spirit and a different Gospel' (see 2 Cor 11: 4).[7]

In the original article, quotations from Dr Rabbitts include supporting references in other works. They are not included here but I urge you to find the article and research the references. She also refers to a Bible known as the Passion Translation, though it is really a paraphrase rather than a translation. The article provides links to various critiques of this Bible and shows its strong connection to the NAR movement.

One evening, pondering the errors in Replacement Theology, Restorationism, Kingdom Now, the Toronto Blessing, the

NAR, and the practice of impartation, I watched a TV program that vividly illustrated their detrimental effects on the church.

Poisoning the Church

After watching a TV documentary[8] on the DuPont scandal, I felt compelled to investigate further. Numerous articles, TV programmes, and online videos have highlighted DuPont's decades-long concealment of the harm caused by chemicals used in its non-stick Teflon™ products. These chemicals poisoned people and the environment, not only in Parkersburg, West Virginia—where DuPont had a Teflon plant—but also worldwide.

The story began in 1951 when DuPont started using a chemical called PFOA, also known as C8, in the manufacturing of Teflon. The Minnesota Mining and Manufacturing Company (3M) invented PFOA and supplied it to DuPont. It was used to keep coatings like Teflon from clumping during production.

Although PFOA was very dangerous, it was not classified as hazardous by the government and did not appear on any list of regulated materials. In 2016, The New York Times reported what had been going on since the 1950s:

... over the decades that followed, DuPont pumped hundreds of thousands of pounds of PFOA powder through the outfall pipes of the Parkersburg facility into the Ohio River.[9]

PFOA-laced sludge was deposited into open, unlined pits where it seeped directly into the ground, entering the water table and contaminating the drinking water of more than 100,000 local residents.

This led to suffering for residents, including DuPont workers and their children, as well as pets, livestock, and wildlife. For humans, exposure to C8 caused various ailments and serious health problems, many of them long term. Pregnant mothers were particularly affected, with birth defects prominently featured in later investigations.

Both DuPont and 3M had been studying the chemical since the 1960s and knew exposure to it could harm human health and cause birth defects, but they kept silent about the dangers and covered up the risks. DuPont continued to manufacture Teflon and dump chemical waste into waterways.

In 2001, residents of the region affected by C8 in their drinking water brought a class-action lawsuit against DuPont. DuPont settled, agreeing to pay the plaintiffs $343 million.

Unconventionally, the plaintiffs refused individual payments and instead established a Science Panel to study the link between C8 in drinking water and human disease.

C8 contamination is so widespread that 99% of Americans have the chemical in their blood, and it has been found in the blood of people worldwide. Though sources of contamination remain unclear, it's believed industrial waste and consumer products that shed C8 over time are the likely causes.

Under the terms of the lawsuit settlement, six water districts were empowered to test people's blood and sue DuPont if exposure to C8 proved to be harmful.

DuPont was confident the test results would prove C8 was safe.

The Science Panel used some of the settlement funds to offer volunteers $400 each, thus encouraging participation in blood sample analysis.

Through the payout and a massive media effort, the panel got more than 70,000 people to participate. The process took more than seven years. In 2012, the results were in: Exposure to C8 in drinking water caused six different human diseases.[10]

The tests revealed links between C8 exposure and kidney cancer, testicular cancer, ulcerative colitis, thyroid disease, pre-eclampsia, and high cholesterol.

The BBC documentary recounts how the testing was carried out to find some 'good blood' in the population to compare with the contaminated blood of those living in the affected area. Researchers searched all over the USA, then the globe, and eventually found uncontaminated blood only in samples from soldiers enlisted during the Korean War. This uncontaminated blood was from a time before DuPont started distributing Teflon.

These poisons have not dissipated and are still being detected all over the earth's surface in the 2020s.

The Chemistry of Deception

As I delved into the DuPont saga, I couldn't help but notice parallels with the church's contamination by the Toronto Blessing and the NAR. This toxic mix has global repercussions, ranging from mild to severe. It's akin to DuPont's cover-up, revealing a lack of investigation and discernment among church leaders.

This poisonous atmosphere affects new church members, just as chemical contamination leads to birth defects. New believers exposed to questionable teachings and practices from Toronto and the NAR might perceive them as acceptable if unaware of biblical teachings. Unbalanced leadership further contributes to the problem.

Like DuPont claimed C8 was safe, Church leaders host NAR speakers without adequately testing their teachings. It appears they deem them safe.

The Old Testament prophet Jeremiah faced a similar problem we face in the Church today. It seems that the people of Israel were not listening to the Lord and had created other ways of following him.

Old Testament history tells us that there were various sources of water. One was the standing water kept in large pits dug into the ground. Others included wells or freshwater lakes. But the best was the fresh, life-giving water that came from underground springs or mountainsides.

God, through Jeremiah, likened the waywardness of the Jews in that day to their stubbornness in continuing to choose the wrong sources:

My people have committed two sins: They have forsaken me, the spring of living water, and have dug their own cisterns, broken cisterns that cannot hold water. (Jeremiah 2.13).

Are we drinking from broken, contaminated cisterns instead of fresh, living water? Or perhaps, because we persist in tolerating these false teachings, we have been *given* poisoned water to drink – (see Jeremiah 8:14). The Church needs fresh, living water but we've gone somewhere and come back with a container of polluted water and then shared it with others (see Jeremiah 2:17-19). We've never known or forgotten or not discerned what the fresh, living water tastes like.

The Road You Leave Behind

As with the vacuous ideas of the hippie movements and the Marxism of the 1960s and 70s I now see the same processes happening in the churches. Nonsensical ideas are being circulated and accepted by gullible Christians who could easily refute them if they took the trouble to examine them and study the scriptures on which they are based.

What on earth happened to the Church?

Back in the 1970s we took that new road I described in Chapter 3. It offered enlightenment and a hope we could all work toward. Restorationism promised much so we took a new route to embrace the dream. Then, in the early 1990s, with church leaders feeling powerless against the onslaught of secularism we saw Toronto, another fork in the road also described in Chapter 3, as a way of bringing revival and re-presenting the Church to the world.

Next came the NAR, which also appeared exciting. But none of these movements were initiated by God, so they never bore any genuine fruit. Nothing occurred that would not have happened through ordinary evangelism and church growth programs had these false teachings never appeared.

When you leave the known road to embark on a different one, you don't know what to expect. It was presented as an adventure with God, but what lay ahead was suspect. It's not overt rebellion against God but seduction and deception that leads us astray, making us believe we're on the right path.

When we – when I – got involved with Restorationism or went to Toronto, either literally or metaphorically, and got caught-up with the NAR, we fooled ourselves. I fooled *my*self. When we let go of purity and embraced what made us feel fashionable, exciting, and progressive, we lost something essential. It is to our detriment that we lost it. And we did not even realise that we *had* lost it. Those other more worldly impulses won over the godly incentives of integrity, diligence, and discernment.

It should have been glaringly obvious to us that, for instance, in going to another part of the world and apparently bringing the Holy Spirit back to fulfil a particular task, revealed something was seriously wrong. The Holy Spirit makes himself graciously available to all, for all tasks in all places. It was and is so very unscriptural.

Why did I, why did we, think it was acceptable to stray from the path the Lord set before us? We should have never left His side.

Drifting Away

This narrative of God's people drifting away and Him, in His faithfulness, working to bring us back repeats itself throughout history, in individual believers' lives, and in the wider church.

We find similar examples in the stories of Israel in the Old Testament. Some tell of Israel's involvement in idolatry, worshipping false gods instead of the true God of Israel. On one notable occasion, this led to them being invaded by an enemy army and many of them being killed or taken into captivity in Babylon.

It is possible that God may send the church into captivity so that we learn lessons, and then come back purified and cleansed of our idolatry, false religion, and false prophecy? Many in the church cannot fathom that God would allow this, not understanding His ways and the purpose of these trials.

A Summary of This Chapter

My investigation of the NAR is not exhaustive but aims to initiate an examination. You will find that the NAR is a blend of truth and misleading distortions, a prime example of a movement of mixture – something God hates. I am not saying that NAR teachers don't ever say anything true or worthwhile. They often do. But isn't that what deception is?

Dr Rabbitts again, from the article referenced earlier:

It is extremely difficult to critique their material without appearing uncharitable towards the truth contained within it. More discerning Christians have therefore tended to be divided by the influence of the NAR - some see the good and are unwilling to throw out the baby with the bathwater. Others reject it completely as outright deception (2 Cor 11: 4). Many are simply fearful of speaking out against a movement that may include things 'of God', in case they accidentally blaspheme the Holy Spirit.[11]

As I have said many times, regarding the various movements, philosophies, and world views I have been describing, I am not disputing the sincerity of those caught up in these things. Whether it is Cultural Marxism or the Toronto Blessing, or the NAR, I urge all believers to think deeply about their beliefs and where they originated. Test everything.

In the conclusion to her study Dr Rabbitts also urges each one of us to bring these things before the Lord:

However, broadly speaking, when NAR teaching and culture is held up to the light of Scripture, it fails virtually every single test. The problem is that it has intermingled with and now suffuses mainstream charismatic Christianity in Britain, which is one reason why so many faithful charismatics find themselves unable to find a sound church fellowship.

The growth of the NAR must be weighed before the Lord, especially in the light of scriptures forecasting deception during the times of the end. I do not believe, however, that 'retreat' is the only option left for faithful believers. A systematic critique is desperately needed and we must search the scriptures carefully to find out the truth, and be ready to defend it, contending earnestly for the faith (Jude 3). If the NAR really is as deceptive as it appears, the future of the Western Church and its witness may just hang in the balance.[12]

With the false teaching of Toronto and the NAR gaining

ground in the churches of the West we must remember Paul's warnings to us and reflect on how relevant they are for us today:

In the presence of God and of Christ Jesus, who will judge the living and the dead, and in view of his appearing and his kingdom, I give you this charge: Preach the word; be prepared in season and out of season; correct, rebuke and encourage with great patience and careful instruction. For the time will come when people will not put up with sound doctrine. Instead, to suit their own desires, they will gather around them a great number of teachers to say what their itching ears want to hear.

They will turn their ears away from the truth and turn aside to myths. But you, keep your head in all situations, endure hardship, do the work of an evangelist, discharge all the duties of your ministry. (2 Timothy 4: 1-5).

My investigations into the NAR are limited, but I hope I've raised awareness of potential dangers. Don't just accept what I write, verify for yourself, check the scriptures, and seek God who is a loving God and wants you to know the truth, understand his ways, and discover where you are in his prophetic timeline.

Notes:

[1] http://uir.unisa.ac.za/handle/10500/15821 last accessed 05.09.18.

[2] See: https://banner.org.uk/res/kt1.html last accessed 11.08.18.

[3] See: https://nelson.ink/excerpts/glory-clouds-bethel/

[4] Find descriptions of how Bible characters fell like dead men or were terrified. Contrast this with these recent encounters where we see people videoing on their mobile phones and whooping!

[5] Hunter, B. (2016), *Off the Map: Bill Johnson and the Pursuit of Extrabiblical Authentication*, Christian Research Institute, Charlotte NC at: https://www.equip.org/articles/off-map-bill-johnson-pursuit-extrabiblical-authentication/

[6] See: https://www.prophecytoday.uk/comment/church-issues/item/1351-the-new-apostolic-reformation-an-overview.html Last accessed 20.08.19

[7] Ibid.

[8] BBC Four, (2019), *Poisoning America – The Devil We Know*. BBC, London. A Storyville Documentary – Broadcast September 2019 See: https://www.bbc.co.uk/programmes/b0bs68rr

[9] New York Times, (2016) *The Lawyer Who Became DuPont's Worst Nightmare* at https://www.nytimes.com/2016/01/10/magazine/the-lawyer-who-became-duponts-worst-nightmare.html Last accessed 27.08.19.

[10] Wilson, J. (20019), *The Devil We Know: How DuPont Poisoned the World with Teflon*, an Organic Consumers Organisation article at: https://www.organicconsumers.org/blog/devil-we-know-how-dupont-poisoned-world-teflon Last accessed 27.08.19.

[11] See: https://www.prophecytoday.uk/comment/church-issues/item/1351-the-new-apostolic-reformation-an-overview.html Last accessed 20.08.19

[12] Ibid.

Chapter 13

WE CLOSE OUR EYES

Under an Illusion

In my early investigations, I attempted to discuss my discoveries with long-time friends from my local church, some of whom I had led in homegroups, and others whose homegroups I had been part of. We had shared various activities over the years, both church-related and otherwise. However, when I broached the issues explored in this book, I encountered a range of reactions that stifled open dialogue.

My initial attempts to share findings began after my trip to Israel, where I became acutely aware of the stark contrast between the situation there and the Western media narrative. This realisation prompted me to delve deeper into related matters, including the New Age movement, Cultural Marxism, Replacement Theology, Toronto, and the NAR. Regrettably, discussions on these topics hit an insurmountable roadblock – a perplexing and disconcerting blindness.

Returning from Israel in early October 2017, I launched into a series of explorations that included an interview with the then leader of the New Church stream I was in. I wanted to know their stance on Replacement Theology, Restorationist and Kingdom Now beliefs. He affirmed that the church stream had a strong adherence to these beliefs while denying the importance of the Jewish people and the land of Israel in current or historical world events and the Bible narrative. He talked about recently travelling to Israel and visiting Christians there whom he called "Palestinians".

A problem with this is that there is no mention in church

meetings about God's purposes for Israel and the Jews, Replacement Theology or Restorationism. That these issues are never named is misleading and upholds the telling of a "noble lie" – an untruth maintained to preserve harmony or advance an agenda. Initially reluctant to accept this, my continued research deepened my concerns. Could church leaders be misleading the congregation with hidden beliefs shaping the church's direction? The absence of discussion on these topics implied their insignificance, subtly teaching by omission – an eloquent silence that speaks volumes.

Nevertheless, a sense of responsibility weighed on me. I felt for the believers within my community, trapped in a bubble of illusion, unaware of the unfolding reality. This idea seemed scarcely credible so, I revisited my doubts, continually seeking truth, sometimes questioning my own sanity, especially after seemingly flawless Sunday church meetings.

We had taken a path unintended by God, ignorant of His attempts to get our attention as the world, and the church, faced divine upheaval. Oddly, this remained unnoticed within the church's atmosphere. No acknowledgment of deception, no remorse for a nation in turmoil, no confession of indifference toward Israel and the Jews – only an apparent unwavering faith in the church's chosen direction. Messages of an impending revival continued to flow from individuals stepping up to the microphone each week, predicting, for example, visions of blazing "fires of Revival."

One of the prophecies given in June 2018 received special attention. It came from a local leader regarded as a Prophet. He said that he "sees three years ahead" and went on to predict a series of exciting, feel-good events that would come during the following three-year period: a "fresh outpouring", a training and raising of leaders some of whom would be sent overseas, "a season of increasing visibility and influence in Bedford". The prophecy included many of the usual NAR buzzwords and phrases that I used to employ: "upgrade", "multiplication", "new phase", "increase" and "acceleration".

I often left meetings bewildered, forced to humble myself and reassess it all. I'm very quick to doubt myself. I can beat myself up, no trouble. But I wanted to know the truth. That was what I was living for. I worked through a checklist of the facts and prayed about each part of the research and seeking I'd done. Every time I did this, it led to a confirmation of the thoughts I'd had and the end of my confusion. I do not wish to criticise church members many of whom work hard, as I did, to keep things ticking over. They are fantastic people trapped in a bad system. Basic Christian tenets stand firm, but insight into other pressing issues is absent. There are strong elements of practical atheism here, a focus on human activities – such as running a new children's club or opening a cafe ministry – while ignoring God's divine plan for the world's last days.

The Persistence of Memory

The misleading situation in the church and my desire to find out why it existed led to much thinking, praying and following a path of logical inquiry.

I could not forget things that had happened and were happening - in the world generally and in the church specifically - (the New Age movement, Cultural Marxism, Replacement Theology, Toronto, and the NAR). As I remembered, I revisited my research several times and concluded that there is clear and compelling evidence for the existence of these movements and the errors in them.

This left me with the pressing question: Why do church leaders remain silent about these forces working against us? Either they were unaware, failed to grasp the causes, or allowed their theology and worldview to dictate their inaction. In any case, these leaders had become blind guides leading the blind. Jesus railed against the religious leaders of his day who were not guiding the people correctly:

... if the blind leads the blind, both will fall into a pit.
(Matt. 15: 14).

Although I did repent later, my cry was very uncharitable at first: let the leaders remain in their world of illusion, if that's what they choose, but the congregation deserve the truth. I pondered the predicament of believers in churches like mine and many others with similar views across the nation. They were trapped in a bubble, their leaders suppressing the truth. How had it come to this?

One of the main factors – playing a pivotal role in this situation – is what I refer to as Generational Loss.

Generational Loss

In the book of Exodus, Moses had to re-educate the Israelites after years of wandering in the wilderness caused them to forget God's teachings. Joshua later led them, but after his death, a new generation emerged that didn't know the Lord or His work:

> *And Joshua the son of Nun, the servant of the Lord, died at the age of 110 years. And they buried him within the boundaries of his inheritance in Timnath-heres, in the hill country of Ephraim, north of the mountain of Gaash. And all that generation also were gathered to their fathers. And there arose another generation after them who did not know the Lord or the work that he had done for Israel.*
> (Joshua 2:8-10).

We have witnessed the pattern of Generational Loss in Western society over many decades and saw awareness of God diminish. The 1960s generation lost touch with faith, and subsequent generations knew even less about it. The same thing has been happening in many churches. Subsequent generations arise each one hearing less and less about the truth of things that matter to God. Eventually they get to the place where I found myself. A world in which I drew much of my understanding of life, the Bible, God, and history, from leaders and a leadership system that has drifted away from the truth.

To understand how this happens, I recalled discussions in the 60s and 70s when people absorbed cultural ideas without realising their origins. These ideas, that later proved detrimental, often came from influencers who considered themselves more enlightened than the public.

One of my pub-debating friends was a drama teacher who had absorbed Marxist ideas while at university. He was staging a performance of the rock musical *Tommy* pioneered by band The Who and was encouraging his pupils to participate. This production contains strong anti-Christian themes and the children taking part would have been influenced by the ideas pervading it. I should imagine very few of them would have had the opportunity to hear anything positive about Christianity because mention of it would have been excluded from discussions.

The same process that brought change then is operating in the church now. Not the ideas and ideologies, although it may include them to some extent, but the process. Most believers, especially the younger generations, don't know or understand where the dominant ideologies come from.

They never saw how, from the 60s and 70s, Restorationism promised great times for the church and, during and since that same period, many promises of imminent revival have been given. They never saw how the Toronto Blessing and other similar movements fed into and perpetuated all these false hopes. The older leaders in the New Churches – and probably most evangelical churches in the West – are failing to be honest about this. They don't discuss these issues but many still believe in them. The impact varies depending on factors like location, demographics, and church leadership. False promises of revival, signs and wonders, and misapplied prophetic promises about creating a Kingdom on earth persist.

Perpetuating this situation has led to the fabrication of a fake world in which believers live and from which they draw much of their understanding of life, the Bible, God, and history.

Life in the Biome

My wife and I lived, with our family in Cornwall, for 16 years. While there we saw how a large, redundant china clay pit was turned into one of the most visited tourist attractions in the UK.

A close family friend worked on the building of the Eden Project two miles from where we lived near St Austell. He got permission to take me on a tour of the construction site. This site now boasts eight huge domes in which biomes are housed. These are different climates that are artificially maintained together with their flora and fauna. Here you can experience the world's largest indoor rainforest or a Mediterranean atmosphere.

It is a marvel of human ingenuity and engineering.

When you are in the rainforest section with its heat and humidity it is amazing to realise that just a metre or so away, outside the dome, a (possibly) cold Cornish day exists. Outside is the real world. But you are in the one produced by human beings rather than the one occurring naturally.

Does your church keep you in a biome that maintains a false understanding of life, the Bible, God, and history? And, if that were the case, would you be aware of it?

This is Water

By getting back to the Bible, seeking God for yourself, and reading one or two of the books I have referred to (see reading list in the Appendix) you can be made aware of any illusions you may have come under.

The writer David Foster Wallace illustrates the illusion phenomenon in his now well-known commencement speech to the graduating class of a US university:

Greetings parents and congratulations to Kenyon's graduating class of 2005.

There are these two young fish swimming along and they happen to meet an older fish swimming the other way, who nods at them and says "Morning, boys. How's the water?" And the two young fish swim on for a bit, and then eventually one of them looks over at the other and goes "What the hell is water?" [1]

In his speech, Wallace explains the notion that the most apparent and vital realities can be the most challenging to perceive and discuss. I, like Wallace, don't intend to come across as a superior, more enlightened figure teaching less mature believers, be it in age or experience. I possess no unique knowledge. My approach was to revisit the Bible, read it in a straightforward manner, and seek God's guidance through prayer. Alongside this, I delved into readily accessible books. The purpose of this narrative is not to portray me as the wise old fish but to emphasise how the most crucial realities are often the most elusive to recognise and articulate.

Notably, Alice Bailey and later proponents of the New Age movement (see section on the New Age Movement in the Appendix) continue to disseminate their ideas, influencing younger generations over extended periods. They carefully exclude contrary belief systems from discourse, making their ideology the dominant culture that successive generations don't question.

A similar process occurs in places where Cultural Marxism is at play, with younger people targeted through academia, the arts, media, and entertainment. Today, Generational Loss is most evident through social media. As the young adopt subversive beliefs, they continue the cycle by influencing others. This perpetuates the neo-Marxist objective of infiltrating Western culture.

The LGBTQ+ movement has also applied this process, following the strategies advocated by the Frankfurt School (see section on Cultural Marxism in the Appendix). Their manual from 1989 guided gays in the arts and media, rapidly advancing the homosexual agenda.[2] The programme has been so effective that in less than three decades the agenda has progressed much more quickly than anyone associated with it could have imagined. Once you understand these tactics, you'll recognise their widespread use and question the reasons behind their success.

Another critical example is the manipulation of truth described in the section about Israel and the Jews. The distortion of truth has advanced the agenda of those seeking Israel's destruction, a process spanning several decades.

People in these and many other groups are unwitting instruments of the devil's plans. Despite this, it is essential to remember that even amid this widespread deception, God continues to work out His plan, and nothing happens outside of His control.

As I observed global events, developments in the West, in our nation, and movements in the churches, my urge to warn others grew. Attempts to engage friends in my local church were often misunderstood. I wasn't sure if anyone would believe or comprehend my message, but I had learned enough to know that silence amounted to betrayal. As part of my investigations, I had come across many other commentators, theologians, church leaders and writers who had discovered the same things I had and were trying to make them known.

In early August 2018, ten months after the Israel trip, I felt a strong compulsion to speak out. My investigations had spanned that time and, although they continue today, I had reached a point then where I thought I too should make known the things I had discovered. I wanted the church stream I was a part of to hear it and hoped it would reach a wider variety of other churches. Several events in my local church strengthened my determination to expose the falsehoods and suppression of truth. I reveal these events in the next chapter.

A Summary of This Chapter

As an "insider," I observed how many churches live in an illusory world fostered by their leadership.

I tried to show how people can, for various reasons, often hear only what they want to hear and disregard other views. Unfortunately, this can mean they sometimes hold on to false ideas while closing their eyes to the truth.

An illusion can exist promoting the belief that everything is going well. There can be a constant stream of prophecies promising good things, while critical issues get ignored. This creates a false sense of security.

The concept of Generational Loss was introduced to explain

how, in controlled environments, successive generations receive a legacy that leads them further from the truth. Young people undergo various church training programmes as part of traditional methods of power exchange and maintaining the status quo.

My investigations highlight other movements discussed in this book and demonstrate how they use similar methods to influence future generations. This phenomenon is also occurring within churches, whether through conscious intent or neglect.

Notes:

[1] Wallace, D. F. (2005), *This is Water*, as quoted on fs. blog at: https://fs.blog/2012/04/david-foster-wallace-this-is-water/ Last accessed 12.10.20.

[2] Kirk, M. and Madsen, H. (1989), *After the Ball: How will America Conquer its Fear and Hatred of Gays in the 90s*, New York, Doubleday.

Chapter 14

THE UNWELCOME SOUND OF AN ALARM

A Sense of Urgency

I was eager to warn others of the danger we were in but unsure of how to proceed. It became clear that I should start locally so I talked with a fellow believer who shared some of my concerns and we agreed to start a new homegroup in which these matters could be discussed.

I went to the weekly church prayer meeting. I believed the 'prayer warriors' would already be aware of faulty teaching and practices and share my concerns but the opposite was true. I got a strong indicator that things were worse and more urgent than I thought.

At the Monday morning meeting, there were about seven of us. One woman exhibited signs of the 'Toronto Twitch,' shaking and jerking as she spoke, while another woman seemed lost in her own world, chuckling and cackling during conversations. I waited for an opportunity to speak, and when the leader asked if anyone had something to share, I gathered the courage to speak up. I introduced myself, detailing my previous involvement in the church, where I actively supported various roles, including being a Junior Church leader, home group leader, and participating in evangelistic events. I mentioned my role in encouraging participation in the signs and wonders and healing ministries of the prophetic movement.

I continued to explain how the Lord's intervention led me to doubt the ideas infiltrating the church which I now saw as deceptive. Although they didn't fully comprehend my concerns, the prayer group prayed about them, which I appreciated.

However, witnessing the display of Toronto-type manifestations which no one in the group questioned, showed the situation had deteriorated. This presented me with a personal challenge because of my own involvement in these behaviours and encouraging others to do the same. I later repented after seeking the Lord's guidance.

Another event pushing me to speak out was the alarming incident when we were told to believe that a revival was being brought to us from South America.

Another Imported Revival

A pastor from a nearby church had visited Bogota, Colombia, in South America, driven by the desire to experience the 'revival' there and bring it back to the UK. He believed this was a genuine move of God and, upon his return, enthusiastically shared a video of himself 'receiving it'.

Being fired-up by the 'anointing' he promptly informed a group of local pastors about his intention to pass it on to other leaders, with hopes that it would influence our region and beyond. Our leaders confirmed his participation in the local church leader's prayer breakfast and described how he had passed it on to those present. During a Sunday morning meeting, one of our leaders, deeply affected by this, expressed the desire to pass it on to our congregation.

I was engrossed in research and investigation into these matters so, I was horrified by this proposal. I asked to speak privately with this elder after the meeting. While trying to reassure him by emphasising my long-standing commitment to the church, I explained my doubts about the practice of impartation, However, my comments received no feedback, and there was no attempt to halt discussions about this new 'revival'.

In fact, for a while, the opposite happened. The local pastor at the centre of it started having mid-week 'revival' meetings at his church. He put on public showings of the Bogota video in which the pastors there, Ricardo and Patricia Rodríguez, had 'prophesied' over him and the other English pastors who had travelled with him. They said things like: *"your nation will explode into revival again. This is a time of God and a wonderful time for England ..."* They also said: *"the flame* (presumably of England's Christianity) *has not gone out. He* (God) *sees an ember of coal, he sees it and the Lord says blow, blow, blow and the flame will ignite again"*. Ricardo blew on him and the English pastors who had travelled with him, and they all fell backwards surrendering to his will while displaying the practice of being 'slain in the spirit'. Other prophecies were spoken over them as they lay on the floor.

I investigated Ricardo and Patricia Rodríguez and the history of the revival in Bogota. The revival itself appeared to be a kind of mass religious hysteria although there will be many needy people involved in it who are genuine seekers after God. And God, in his mercy, will meet with them. This is the same pattern we find in the Toronto blessing and at NAR events.

Who were the people who inspired Rodríguez's movement? Where did these Colombian pastors get their motivation from?

It would not take anyone even with limited resources and research skills very long to discover the answer. The easy-to-find articles and video clips reveal they have received 'anointings' from the likes of Benny Hinn, Cindy Jacobs, and Bill Hamon; all highly regarded apostles and prophets in the signs and wonders and NAR movements.

One would expect church leaders to scrutinise the origins of this expected revival, but the lack of discussion indicated otherwise. This repeated pattern of accepting spurious promises from Restorationism, Kingdom Now teaching, the Toronto Blessing, and now the NAR, brings nothing but false hope to the believers in our nation and the West.

There was no revival.

The excitement and hope faded quickly, and no explanations were offered to the congregations. The entire episode, along with other false promises, was swept under the carpet, to the detriment of believers in our town and further afield. I could see the false teaching having a devastating effect. And I could see that, combined with increasing hostility from society in general, these things would all bring irreversible consequences. Believers needed to be aware. Not to be afraid but to be prepared.

The rise of anti-Christian sentiment in our society, fuelled by Cultural Marxism, and the infiltration of New Age and interfaith movements in the churches was not being recognised. The church's ongoing alignment with the changing culture could lead to its complete absorption. True believers will be faced with the dilemma of staying in their current fellowship or seeking Bible-believing, truth-loving fellowship elsewhere.

This situation reminded me of my childhood experience, stranded on a sandbank in the River Thames as the tide rushed in. The overwhelming body of water, laden with the weight of the North Sea and English Channel, is forced into the narrowing estuary. Once the tide turned, it surged rapidly, and those not vigilant were at risk of being trapped. This analogy accurately reflects the state of the church today, and it serves as the central theme of this book.

Impelled to Speak

The compulsion to tell my fellow believers was becoming burdensome. There was much to convey, and I'm not the most articulate person. I needed to shape this message for clarity and avoid overwhelming hearers. My goal was to sound an alarm.

I wanted to share the message of God's immense love for all His children, but also the necessity of His corrective guidance. This reminded me of the moments when I first entered His presence years before in a humble seaside town. The brief period of divine anger was quickly replaced by a mixture of sadness that I had strayed, followed by overwhelming feelings of forgiveness and mercy as I repented and resolved to change.

The parallels were striking. We had veered off the path God intended, embracing various false teachings from those claiming to speak on His behalf. We failed to exercise discernment, putting ourselves in great peril.

Jesus warned that deception would be one of the most

significant signs of His return, and it would emanate from those claiming to be Christians, as He put it, those coming "in my name" (see Matthew 24: 3-5). He urged us to "watch and pray" regarding end-time events (Matt. 24: 42-44), but we had not been vigilant. The troubling events in the world today align with Jesus' descriptions in Matthew 24, signalling the early signs of these prophesied events.

Nipped in the Bud

In charismatic church meetings, members can approach the front, often during the worship, to address the congregation. During my active involvement in the signs and wonders movement, I frequently delivered prophecies and 'words of knowledge.'

One Sunday morning, I attempted to share my growing understanding of the concerns detailed in this book with the congregation. A leader asked for a brief outline of my message, and as I began to describe it, a strange, visceral awareness came over me. I suddenly knew that, despite being a previously trusted member, I would not be allowed to deliver the message for the congregation to judge. Although the message conveyed God's immense love, it emphasised the need for correction, with a hint of God's anger and deep sadness at our waywardness. Permission to deliver the message was denied.

A few days later, I was summoned to a meeting with two church leaders to discuss the message. I attended, notebook in hand, eager to hear their views. They did not grasp my concerns and focused on the part of the message that spoke of God's anger rather than His love and His desire for us to be back in the centre of His will. Although love was, and is, the central theme of my message, they were fearful of any mention of God's anger.

My focus was on the dangers associated with embracing the false teachings I have outlined earlier in this book. I aimed to highlight signs indicative of the end times, such as the return of the Jews to their Promised Land. However, my warnings were met with resistance. It became clear that my message would not find a platform in future church gatherings due to the concern that it might sway some individuals. This revealed a deeper worry that my perspective could disrupt the church. I realised I should accept the situation rather than try to alter it.

One of the leaders, dismissive of my concerns, was itching to leave. When he went, the other person prepared to wind up the meeting and at that point, I was advised to "become a Berean" although I had made it clear that for months, I had been doing exactly that.

"That went well," I joked to myself as I left, but my humour masked my emotions. I felt disheartened and embarrassed. I must have got it all wrong. I resolved to investigate their remarks and the Bible teachers they had recommended. The home group I had intended to establish with my friend was prohibited.

At that juncture, having been engaged in a new round of Christian media ministry for over a year, I had heard numerous stories from believers grappling with similar issues in their respective churches. Affected by newly introduced false teachings in the churches they had attended for years, they were struggling with the idea of leaving. Requests for information were coming in from individuals and small groups facing comparable challenges in their regions. They wanted to meet with others for support. This underscored a hunger for God's Word amid a waning belief in the authority of Scripture. I was reminded of the rector in the Anglican church I formerly attended, who contended with the leadership of his time, endeavouring to realign them with God's path.

I share these experiences to provide insight to those who may confront similar obstacles. If you harbour similar concerns and are endeavouring to address comparable situations within your church community, perceive this as a forewarning of potential hurdles you may encounter. Do not despair; you are not alone, assistance is available.

Upon scrutinising the leaders' assertions and recommendations, I came to the realisation that I had erred in doubting myself. I concluded that in certain churches, dissenting voices are suppressed, and their views dismissed. They may be branded as biased, and their viewpoints disregarded.

In various talks and preaches I'd heard in my local church over the years, subtle exhortations were made urging the congregation to adhere to the teachings they were receiving and refrain from seeking alternative perspectives because deviating could result in adopting fallacious or eccentric beliefs or being taken in by conspiracy theories. I am convinced that the leaders espousing these notions do not intend to instil fear in their listeners deliberately; rather, they are so deeply entrenched in their misconceptions that they genuinely believe they are acting in the right manner.

Following this meeting, any aspirations for future leadership roles or a desire to prophesy would be thwarted, as I would always seek to propagate the message that had become my conviction and an integral part of my life. As I delved deeper into it, my eagerness to proclaim it intensified.

I already possessed most of the material constituting my message – the themes addressed in this book – in note form. Since verbal expression of my concerns was unfeasible, I resolved to commit them to writing, with the aim of producing leaflets, stimulating discussions, and connecting with fellow believers.

This type of action can be daunting due to the prevalent fear in many churches that questions or challenges to leaders may disrupt God's order. However, as individual believers or small groups, we should not be afraid to seek God for answers ourselves. Scripture is accessible to ordinary believers, and the Holy Spirit provides guidance and understanding (see 1 John 2:20-21). Believers are Holy Spirit taught.

You may often hear people today saying that it is hard to interpret Scripture correctly, but Jesus never, ever said anything like that, quite the opposite. He often said things like "have you not read ..." or "haven't you read in the scriptures ..." or "you are wrong because you don't know the scriptures". He talked mostly to untrained, common people and always assumed that any blame for misunderstanding any teaching of Scripture is not to be placed on the Scriptures themselves, but on those who misunderstand or fail to accept what is written. Further to this, we see clearly that most of the New Testament is written, not to church leaders, but to entire congregations. Concerns over the practices in some of the New Churches caused me to question the belief maintained in them that they are churches built on New Testament principles.

A New Testament Church?

Teaching in the early church typically occurred in believers' homes or Jewish synagogues and took the form of a discussion or debate in which everyone participated. Today, in older, traditional, or established churches, calling out a question during a sermon would be unthinkable. The clergyman presiding over the congregation speaks, and everyone listens, accepting his words as truth due to his position and his attire.

In newer churches, it has been suggested that questions during sermons are permissible, but there is no evidence of this occurring. Certain leaders may rise in prominence, becoming venerated and beyond questioning by the congregation. They effectively replace the vicar figure of older churches, wearing their unassailable authority like a clerical collar. The old way of listening to the preacher and simply accepting what is said has remained. The congregation prefers it this way, believing the leader has "figured it out" so they do not have to do anything.

Over the years, I have visited many 'New' churches (or those with similar aspirations) and find it remarkable how many have adopted practices like the Anglican church I used to attend years ago. Although often adhered to just as closely, the liturgy in 'New' churches is unwritten.

Another deviation from New Testament practices is the tight control leaders exert over prophetic utterances. The Bible indicates that those bringing prophetic messages should be allowed to speak, with others assessing the message's nature and significance (see 1 Cor. 14:29-33).

I will not go into this subject further here, as it has already been amply written about elsewhere, and suitable publications are suggested in the Appendix.

I don't have the space here to detail the significant differences between early church practices depicted in the Bible and the practices in the New Churches. For instance, there is no evidence in the New Testament that groups of believers owned large buildings or employed numerous salaried leaders and staff. Even Paul had to work part-time to support himself.

When I first began to question the happenings in the churches of Britain, my thoughts turned to my Catholic upbringing. Shortly after my conversion, I realised that many of the beliefs in that church were formed, not on the Bible, but on its traditions.

Many churches in the West have developed belief systems not based on the Bible but on their own interpretations of it. Over many years, these have developed into accepted ways of believing and doing things. They are now so deeply entrenched that change is difficult or unlikely.

In the 1980s, I witnessed New Churches forming as a breakaway from established churches due to a belief that unnecessary traditions hindered their mission. They sought to create something fresh and new. However, today they are encumbered by other traditions and practices, mirroring the old traditional churches they once sought to escape.

A Summary of This Chapter

I have a message that needs to be heard, discussed, and weighed. It might be wrong, so a dialogue is crucial. My voice was silenced, sparking a desire to reach out to all believers, not only in the New Churches but other churches in the nation. Time is running short so, I chose to convey this message through a book. The few leaflets I originally had in mind would not have been able to contain it.

I was reminded of Jeremiah's experience in Jeremiah Chapter 36. While I don't claim to be a Prophet, have a prophetic ministry, or compare myself to Jeremiah, some similarities exist.

Jeremiah faced false prophets who predicted a great future, contrasting with his message of disaster without repentance.

Jeremiah was banned by those in power from talking to the ordinary people so he wrote out his message and sent it to be read out in a public place where everyone could hear it. The message, written on a scroll, was eventually brought to the king, and read to him. Each time a section of the message was read out to the king he cut it off the scroll and burned it in a fire. He, and his advisors, showing no fear of God, rejected the message. (v.24). The king commanded that Jeremiah and his colleague be arrested but the Lord protected them, and they escaped.

Some people in attendance, however, did fear God and urged caution but their words were not heeded (v. 25). God told Jeremiah to write it all out again. This could have taken over a year if you see how long it took to write the first one (compare verse 1 with verse 9) and therefore the whole story could have been played out over a period of anything up to 3 years. It has taken me a comparable length of time to get the message of this book to its first draft and much more detail has been included than if I had spoken for a few minutes in a church meeting. I have been able to add much more just as Jeremiah did, (see verse 32).

The rebuff led me to deeper research and understanding of the message's importance. It drove me to a greater dependency on God by showing me my own inadequacy without his help. I hope you won't disregard the message. I urge caution if you decide to reject it. Read, test, study, verify the facts, and, above all, evaluate it against Scripture. Pray for insight, for I believe God will provide it.

Chapter 15

THE DECLINE OF PROPHETIC MINISTRY

The Rareness of Litmus

As evident in previous chapters, the prophetic ministry in Western churches has taken a troubling turn. I'm specifically referring to the practice of the gift of prophecy and the role of the Prophet as outlined in the Bible.

There's also been a failure to instil a strong belief in the prophetic scriptures, both in the Old Testament and the New. While these scriptures may occasionally be discussed, they're often presented as lessons for life application rather than as literal predictions of future events.

In terms of the operation of prophetic gifts and ministries, we've already observed self-proclaimed prophets freely moving through our churches, delivering prophecies that fail to materialise. Despite their track record, they're allowed to host seminars and instruct others on becoming prophets. Since the 1970s, the New Churches have emphasised prophetic ministry, which is not inherently problematic. However, this emphasis makes it more susceptible to counterfeits.

With the resurgence of this gift during the charismatic renewal, one would expect to see increased emphasis on mature spiritual discernment and teachings that help church members distinguish between genuine and counterfeit prophecies.

In my recent experience, the sole criterion for assessing prophecy is whether it aligns with the prevalent ideology of imminent revival and the leadership's view on various interpretations of scripture.

Where Did We Go Wrong?

The teachings on prophetic gifts I received during the Training for Supernatural Ministry course exhibited a lack of awareness about deception and relied on the same criteria for evaluating prophetic words: does it align with current ideas? Techniques taught, like prophesying while blindfolded, were susceptible to deception.

Why do the leaders of these "Schools of the Prophets" courses show such a lack of integrity on this matter? The notion that someone can choose to become a prophet is quite preposterous when considering the biblical accounts of how prophets were called, operated, and were regarded. Prophets conveyed God's sentiments about the behaviour of His people, focusing on obedience and the consequences of disobedience. It was not a casual desire. They were often compelled to share unwelcome messages.

However, if you aspire to "move in the prophetic" within a New Church setting, you need not concern yourself with such matters. Just ensure your prophecies contain only warm, uplifting words or temporary encouragement for believers.

When prophecy is abused in this manner, it becomes nothing more than empty platitudes. Does God always communicate in this manner? Sometimes, a true word from God filled with His love includes challenging aspects, such as predictions of difficult times ahead, rebukes, or calls to change direction.

I've witnessed individuals uproot their entire lives – family, job, career, children's education, and more – due to prophecies that later proved false. In places where this misapplication of prophecy is widespread, some may offer "words from God" in the middle of conversations. These "words" often consist of positive messages, such as promises of prosperity or healing, and merely reflect the speaker's well-intentioned desires for the recipient, without necessarily hearing from God. However, if such a "word" comes from a church leader, the issue of integrity arises. In some churches where prophetic utterances are commonplace, leaders instruct regular contributors to "bring a word of encouragement" to lend credibility to the proceedings. The consequences of this misuse of prophecy are significant. It leads to a diminished perception of the prophetic gift's importance and its trustworthiness. Instead of anticipation and excitement when a "prophetic word" is delivered in a meeting, there's often a prevailing sense that most of the congregation has lost interest.

"God Told Me ..."

Claiming in a church meeting or personal setting that your words are a message from God is a grave matter. While Paul instructs us not to despise prophecy, I urge caution. Repeating numerous prophecies is not indicative of spiritual maturity. It's possible to be deceived about the source of a prophecy, as I've demonstrated. (See Matt. 7:15-23.)

In a 2017 article, Josh Buice critiqued the increasingly common habit of often saying "God told me ..." within Christian circles. He contends that this type of language undermines the sufficiency of scripture and takes God's name in vain.[1]

If you want to witness evidence of dubious prophecies, look no further than the signs and wonders movement and the New Apostolic Reformation (NAR). In the US, signs and wonders ministries abound, and some have extended to the UK. For instance, the Glasgow Prophetic Centre offers features like "The Elijah List," a magazine-style website that I once subscribed to during my misguided days. It sends out daily prophecies for readers to digest.

This approach is unscriptural and is akin to reading a horoscope in a newspaper or magazine. These individuals are essentially saying, "God told me ...".

The internet is teeming with self-proclaimed prophets and apostles who frequently claim to hear God speaking to them, see visions, are visited by angels, or are transported to heaven. This often bewilders "ordinary Christians."

I don't have the time or space to delve deeply into what genuine biblical prophecy entails. I recommend that you explore this for yourself and refer to some of the books recommended in the Appendix. However, avoid using books associated with the NAR or the Bethel School of Ministry, unless you're studying matters of error in these subjects.

Being a Light

In our pursuit of the reinstatement of genuine prophetic ministry, we must recognise the importance of God speaking through His church to society, warning of moral, social, and economic consequences and impending divine judgment when His standards are violated.

However, many in the churches of the West do not believe in the church having a prophetic voice in the world or the need for warning of judgment. This view is prevalent not only in our local church but also throughout most evangelical churches.

Yet, a church with these views may struggle to call a nation back to God and His standards. We are not to judge and yet, while we may not be directly responsible for society's behaviour, we have a duty to give fair warning about the ramifications of ignoring God. It is scriptural to speak into and pray for the nation.

Furthermore, our silence can be seen as consent. We must question why anyone, or anything would want the church to remain silent on moral issues and societal matters. In the Old Testament, God's people Israel, were called to be a light to the nations, but it seems that our contemporary New Churches have abandoned this responsibility despite Replacement Theology's inherent notion that the church is the *New* Israel.

Mending the Broken

As we address this problem and seek a return to genuine prophetic ministry, it's evident that we've become spiritually hard of hearing. Decades of unfulfilled promises and lightweight, feel-good messages have left us with lowered expectations of hearing from God and an inability to truly listen to Him.

To mend what's broken, we need to turn to the Bible and learn how the Prophets of old came into God's presence and heard from Him. This was quite unlike the false Prophets of Jeremiah's day. God had stern words for them:

I did not send these prophets, yet they have run with their message;
I did not speak to them, yet they have prophesied.
But if they had stood in My council, they would have proclaimed My words to My people and would have turned them from their evil ways and deeds. (Jer. 23:21-22).

Some New Churches offer seminars and 'Schools of the Prophets,' but if we seek an easy solution without establishing a true relationship with God, these methods won't bring about the necessary change.

False prophecy is harmful, deceiving and misleading God's people, building false hopes and becoming a stumbling block to God's word. Discernment among church members is impaired due to the adulation of leaders, making their teaching unquestionable. Some leaders may not be deliberately deceiving, but their deep involvement in false teaching leads them astray.

Predictions of good times and revival without widespread repentance are founded on shaky ground, rooted in man-made ideas of Restorationism, Kingdom Now, and the NAR. Instead of this, we should base our understanding on a prayerful study of God's ways and a firm belief in the prophetic scriptures in the Bible.

We need to see false prophecy for what it really is; Jeremiah, in his clash with one of the false prophets of his day was quite clear about it:

You have preached rebellion against the LORD
(Jer. 28:15-16).

Knowing God

To truly understand God's character and ways, we must engage in a thorough study of the entire Word of God while approaching it with reverence. This approach allows us to unearth aspects of God's character rarely spoken about and reveals that He cannot be encapsulated by simple "promise verses." Our understanding must evolve, enabling us to discern His divine character behind His actions, leading to substantial and authentic prophetic messages.

In hindsight, I realise phrases like "God is good, all the time" often uttered in church settings were simplistic notions that have developed over time. I believe God *is* good all the time but, when constantly parroted, these ideas depict a somewhat distorted view of God, one we present to appeal to others and often omit the themes of impending judgment and hell. We want to present a nice friendly god, especially to visitors, because we want to be liked but we do not want to mention the coming judgement and certainly not hell. We need to remind ourselves and others of the terror of the Lord:

> ... *knowing therefore the terror of the Lord, we persuade men*, (2 Cor 5:10-11).

Idolatry

The amalgamation of the aforementioned ideas and teachings has engendered a skewed perception of God within Western churches. This may be perpetuated by leaders fearing that conveying the truth could diminish attendance and membership. Yet, this misunderstanding results in a God-fearing void in churches.

The god of most churches in the western world does not appear to be the same God as found in the Bible. He has always wanted to be known as the God of Abraham, Isaac, and Jacob (that's the Jacob who was re-named Israel), and he has not changed.

We must recognise that this false perception of God can be seen as a form of idolatry. It's not the traditional idol of physicality but rather an inaccurate portrayal of God that has been shaped by erroneous teachings and concepts. This idolatrous mindset has been perpetuated for decades, and the root of this error is exposed throughout this book. As I investigated all the issues raised, I saw that we have created a different God, a different Jesus.

This Jesus has reneged on his promises to his ancient people Israel. He has also gone back on his promises regarding the land of Israel.

This Jesus is constantly promising a remarkable revival that never happens.

This Jesus is a nice friendly one who would never judge the world or discipline the church.

This Jesus has changed his views on current sinful behaviour and lifestyles.

I could go on, but I think you get the picture. False ideas about God are not unique but they all have something in common: they all come from human minds. Similarly, recent notions about God have created an idol within many Western churches. On this basis I maintain that most of the churches in the West practice idolatry.

With Replacement Theology, and the idea that God does not keep his promises, doubt was cast on the Bible's narrative, leading to scepticism from "progressive Christians" regarding the creation story, the Flood, the judgment of Sodom and Gomorrah, and Bible prophecy. Due to our inability to comprehend God, we fashioned a different one. With Restorationist and Kingdom Now thought came the idea that we, the church, can create the Kingdom of God on earth.

A Summary of This Chapter

The Bible warns us not to despise prophecy. I do not despise prophecy and I do not think it wrong if someone speaks with confidence when they believe they have heard from God. I simply ask that we understand where false prophecies come from, reject them, test all prophecies, and hold on to what is good.

It is godly discernment I am calling for, (1 Thess. 5: 20-21).

When Jesus returns and sets up his kingdom reign on earth, he will cleanse Israel, other nations and (what was) the Church from their defilements. He will get rid of all the deceptive false prophets along with their doctrines of demons.

There is a spirit of impurity and idolatry in the church. The facilitators of this are the false prophets, but the spiritual power behind it is demonic. These spirits empower and enthuse the false prophets. They hate God and holiness. They drive their victims into moral impurity or indifference about moral issues. And they create false religion. See Zechariah 13: 1- 6 for a description of how God feels about false prophets.

How will he eventually treat those who have misrepresented the truth? With the NAR and the signs and wonders movements we see all these false beliefs converging to create a god most prefer to relate to; one we have brought down to our level and reshaped. This convergence is taking place all over the world, inside the church and outside of it, and at an ever-increasing speed.

Notes:
[1] Buice, J. (2017), *Please Stop Saying "God Told Me"*, on g3min.org at https://g3min.org/stop-saying-god-told-me/ Last accessed 26 July 2019.

Chapter 16

CONVERGENCE

The Need to be Relevant

As the West loses its Judeo-Christian heritage and the collapsing culture becomes more pagan, true believers will feel more and more like exiles in this Postmodern, post-Christian environment.

It looks too late to make a difference in the public sphere so, some are asking: How should we share the Gospel in such a world? In answering, some are proposing we change the Gospel message and move to a new unifying religion they see emerging. I ask: could a postmodern Emerging Church be the forerunner to a religion of tolerance that will cause many believers to fall away and welcome in a One World Religion under the Antichrist?

What is Convergence?

Convergence is a process whereby things come together. In the context of the issues raised in this book, it means various movements and beliefs that, previously, may not have had anything in common finding compromise. Things gradually change, sometimes over decades, and people begin to develop a shared purpose. Secular organisations such as the UN, the WEF and the WHO are joining hands with the New Age movement and various 'liberation' movements, environmental groups, LGBTQ+ and gender identity movements. They are being joined by ecumenical and inter-faith organisations to form a globally awakened group of adherents to a new spirituality.

We can see this happening in our global society, but these ideas are increasingly being forced upon and accepted by the

Church. The reasons given for accepting compromise are often presented as very noble: world peace and 'saving the planet' for example. The dominant philosophy now is that we are all different but let's not hang on to any differences that might disturb the harmony. We should seek Unity with Diversity. Tolerance and the inclusion of all peoples, regardless of race, creed, sexual orientation, and lifestyle should not hinder this.

Religion gets the blame for many of the wars, past and present, so we are told that, as 'good Christians', we have a responsibility to work towards religious unity and peace. This, of course, is propaganda. The hidden agenda is to unite people under one religion so that they will peacefully accept a one-world government. To those, in or out of the church system, who have no real faith in Jesus and no Holy Spirit to guide them this aim will appear to be a logical step in an evolutionary process. This is part of God's plan as the Bible makes clear:

For God has put it in their hearts to execute His purpose by having a common purpose, and by giving their kingdom to the beast, until the words of God will be fulfilled.
(Rev 17:17 (NASB).

Seduction
The danger facing churches, particularly those seeking global revival and the establishment of a kingdom on earth now, lies in being seduced by the convergence process and viewing it as the fulfilment of their dreams, as it shares remarkable similarities.

A striking example of how the New Churches and the NAR can be lured by the false Kingdom Now concept occurred in 2014 when a special envoy was dispatched by the Pope to seek Evangelical support in the US.

Tony Palmer, a Jesuit priest, and personal friend of Pope Francis delivered a video message from the Pope at a Charismatic Evangelical Leadership Conference hosted by American Charismatic Kenneth Copeland, an NAR leader.

The Pope's message emphasised brotherhood, unity, and the declaration that the Reformation protest had ended. After the presentation and video message, Copeland prayed for the Pope and sent a message back. According to Palmer and the Pope, the Protestant Church no longer exists; we are all Catholics again, but Reformed Catholics. Palmer suggested increasing resources for this 'Counter Reformation.' He also promoted the idea that spiritual experience, not doctrine, should unite us, and that the Protestant church must return to the Mother Church (Rome).

This message of unity continued with Palmer releasing a video titled "The Miracle of Unity Has Begun," explaining Pope Francis's message as one of 'brotherhood' where 'our brother' is considered the 'real Bread' and 'real Communion.' This misuse of Christian doctrine threatens to lead us into a false unity.

Following this, Copeland took a delegation to Rome, leading to the establishment of the Kairos Conference in the US in October 2017. Numerous Evangelical pastors either attended or endorsed its goals, with various NAR ministries represented, and Bethel Church providing music and leading worship.

During the Conference, Copeland dismissed the Reformation as a demonic 'church split' and advocated the reunification of one body based on the appeal to Evangelicals from the Pope. He read from a paper written in October 1999 when representatives of the Catholic and Lutheran Churches gathered in Salzburg, Germany and signed a joint declaration about justification.

The declaration ended: *"together, we confess by grace alone, in faith, and Christ's saving work, and not because of any merit on our part, we are accepted by God, and receive the Holy Spirit who renews our heart while equipping and calling us to good and His works"*. This sounds theologically correct but, because many in the Roman Catholic church still believe in salvation by works, the wording of this statement appears to leave room for them to continue in that belief. Questions remain about their devotion to Mary, praying to 'saints,' transubstantiation, and indulgences.

Invoking the ethos of Kingdom Now thinking Copeland encouraged the Conference delegates to embrace this new unity and see it as part of a global revival that will empower the Church to evangelise the world and, as he put it, "get the job done".

Simultaneously, the Pope toured the world, advocating the merging of all religions into one. This might galvanise the Kingdom Now camp's aspirations of 'getting the job done' because, as they see their vision of establishing heaven on earth falter, this offers a potential means to realise their dreams.

Under Pressure

Many leaders of Western church denominations have succumbed to societal pressures.

Bible teachers, church and ministry leaders are beguiled by the notion that they must be part of the (false) unity to prove their relevance in society. Trusted ministers seem to be falling under this spell, raising doubts about their true Christian faith.

This spiritual decay permeates other areas of belief and behaviour, as traditional denominations and New Church streams increasingly adopt secular views and align with society. The church's witness to the nation diminishes as this process accelerates, an unstoppable tide sweeping the church away.

For instance, Archbishop of Canterbury, Justin Welby, endorses membership of the Coexist Foundation, a multi-faith organisation. Numerous such organisations operate at local, national, and global levels.

Criticism of these groups can seem unkind, as many of them do good works alongside their unity goals. Some profess faith in Jesus, although it's challenging to reconcile this with their multi-faith beliefs. Some commentators and Christian pastors have argued, "Well, they love Jesus, so what does it matter?"

Falling Away

Jesus prophesied a falling away from him in the last days (Matthew 24:10). When he said this, he was obviously referring to those in the church because you can't fall away from something you didn't believe in in the first place.

This warning is echoed in scripture:

For the time will come when people will not put up with sound doctrine. Instead, to suit their own desires, they will gather around them a great number of teachers to say what their itching ears want to hear. They will turn their ears away from the truth and turn aside to myths.

(1 Timothy 4:1 and 2 Timothy 4:3-4).

To sharpen our understanding of this process we can swap "put up with" for the word "tolerate". In my local area I have seen whole families – young families – leave church and not attend anywhere else because they can no longer tolerate the truth of scripture.

Will departing from the faith mean that many people will stop attending churches? Not necessarily. It is possible to carry on being a member of a local church or a national church stream – even being very active in that role – but to have departed from the faith. Many are turning to a more open-minded New Spirituality, embracing interfaith dialogue, ecumenism, neo-paganism or a universalism/'Wider Mercy' doctrine (everyone experiences some kind of salvation at some time in the future even if they are not Christian because a loving God would not send anyone to hell).

This spiritual decay is spreading, as traditional and new churches adopt secular views, hastening their assimilation into society, to the detriment of orthodox believers and the church's witness.

An example of departing from the faith could mean that while being part of a local church you follow false ideas such as those espoused by the Emerging Church movement.

The Emerging Church

The motivations of liberal emergent church leaders revolve around recurring themes. They believe the church must adapt to a changing culture and often react negatively to conservative evangelicals who hinder this evolution. Their focus is on the present, emphasising social justice, poverty alleviation, disease prevention, environmental conservation, and religious unity, rather than saving individuals from eternal judgment.

In the historic, established churches it is relatively easy to see the rejection of orthodox beliefs because they are becoming apostate in discernible ways. The pressure to conform to postmodern views on homosexuality and transgender issues, abortion, and feminist issues, on race and ethnicity conflicts means that many leaders feel they must capitulate or be labelled as bigoted and judgemental.

The enemy employs similar tactics in Evangelical, Pentecostal, and charismatic streams, albeit with some variations. New Churches, distancing themselves from traditional 'Churchianity,' have become proud of their success in attracting younger generations. But are they relying more on being relevant than being Biblical?

A Summary of this Chapter.

Convergence is occurring not only in religious and spiritual circles but also in many aspects of our global society. Financial institutions, trade consortiums, the United Nations, global security organisations, climate control bodies, peace groups, interfaith movements, and global development agencies are collaborating to address world issues. In some places, they are succeeding.

The New Age Movement is likely to align with NAR and Kingdom Now adherents due to overlapping beliefs. Together, they seek to bring a form of heaven to earth. But are we usurping God's role in trying to bring about a heaven on earth?

There is clear evidence of this mindset within New Churches and other Western churches. Overconfident rationalism, human conceit, and arrogance seem to characterise these groups, leading them to declare, "We can do it!" or even, "We *are* doing it!" This form of restorationism is essentially humanism—the belief that humanity can establish peace and usher in God's reign on earth.

Sadly, these ideas persist in many churches, despite being contradicted by reality. Parts of the Church remain stuck on a sandbank of false beliefs, and a powerful incoming tide of things much worse, unnoticed by many, threatens to sweep them away. Rescue is within reach, but will they grasp it?

Chapter 17

A SUMMARY OF THIS BOOK

Corralled

This book warns against becoming trapped on a sandbank, facing an unstoppable tide. For the world, this sandbank consists of empty, man-made philosophies and beliefs, some of which I've mentioned in this book. For the church, the sandbank comprises an additional set of beliefs relevant only to Christians, i.e., most people outside the church will be unaware of them and may struggle to understand them.

I began describing this sandbank by depicting society from the 1950s to the 1970s and how cultural movements shifted Western lifestyles and belief systems. I shared my encounter with Jesus and subsequent lifestyle change, highlighting that this happened outside and away from any church.

Focussing on a description of the sandbank more relevant to believers, I recounted my experiences in various church settings, cautioning against the confusion that may arise when zeal for spreading the Gospel intertwines with promoting the aims of a particular church or church stream, especially if tainted by false teachings. Over the years, I fell victim to Replacement Theology, Restorationism, Kingdom Now teaching, the Toronto 'Blessing,' and, finally, the movement variously known as the prophetic movement, the Apostolic and Prophetic movement, and more recently, the New Apostolic Reformation (NAR).

I showed how Restorationism never truly occurred when I first got involved, despite the enthusiasm in the 1980s and 90s. I maintain that it is not happening now and will not happen because it is not the true restoration the Bible speaks of. It is based on incorrect interpretations of scripture that have led to a wrong view of God's eternal plans, including a refusal to admit that the Jewish people and the nation of Israel still have a place in these plans.

I have shown how the NAR has ensnared many Christians, drawing them into a union with inter-faith groups, the New Age movement, and others. I examined the trend in Western churches where certain parts of the Bible, particularly prophetic scriptures, are downgraded, casting doubt on the reliability of many other parts of the Bible.

I've spent considerable time analysing and attempting to define the silence from church leaders on crucial matters, especially those related to God's plan for these last days, suggesting a demonic influence diverting attention away from it. The mishmash of false beliefs perpetuated by misguided leaders has corralled the church into a place where they are in danger of being completely deceived and swept away.

I make deliberate allusions to how the deceptions inherent in the 1960s and 70s societal changes, through cultural Marxism and New Age thought, have parallels in various movements and beliefs in the churches today. Not so much in the beliefs themselves but in the way they are upheld and passed on to others. We will always have those who aspire to lead, whether an individual or a small group, who think they know better than the rest of us, do not fully explain what is driving them, and will attempt to hoodwink us into supporting their hopes and dreams.

Early in my investigations, I realised the dangers the church faced and tried to sound the alarm. My attempts were thwarted, leaving me uncertain and apprehensive. I returned to God with my insecurities, embarking on a deeper quest to understand these dangers and gain greater assurance of my convictions.

Researching and writing about these issues have forced me to think deeply, pray, and verify everything.

I have seen leaders cherry-pick Bible verses to support their positions but there is no benefit in reflection when one is merely justifying preconceived beliefs. However, thoughtful engagement with biblical texts and their contexts can challenge previously held assumptions and provide new insights.

All reflections should lead to some form of transformation. This might include specific actions we need to implement or a renewed understanding of self, of God, or our spiritual experience, all of which should influence future thinking and action. Roughly five years into this investigative journey, I am now more convinced than ever about our place in God's plan of history.

Can The Church Be Rescued?

In my real-life account of being stranded on a sandbank with school friends, I described our miraculous rescue. However, we cannot assume that rescue is inevitable. Is it too late for the church to be delivered?

A point of no return was reached for the people in Noah's time, with only eight saved out of the entire world's population. Similarly, in Sodom and Gomorrah, only a few were rescued.

The Jews in the times of Jeremiah and Isaiah also faced a point of no return. Despite warnings from the prophets about Israel's departure from God, idolatry, and disbelief, the message was rejected. Isaiah had to proclaim that it was too late; they would continue to hear without understanding and see without perceiving. They reached a state where belief became impossible (see Isaiah Chapter 6). When Isaiah asked God how long he should deliver this message, God instructed him to persist until judgment came and the cities lay in ruins, the land became deserted, and the people taken into captivity.

The Church may be so misled by false teachings and idolatry that we fail to recognise our errors, rendering us incapable of repentance and change. In such cases, God may allow us to go into exile to address the issue. Just as the Jews experienced exile in Jeremiah's time, we too may face captivity. Our exile could include various forms of persecution, such as being banished from any meaningful role in society. During the Babylonian captivity, some of God's people aligned themselves with the false gods and evil practices of their captors. When the opportunity arose to return to their promised land, many chose to stay. Some Christians might do the same, finding it easier to become part of an apostate global religion rather than face oppression.

However, during the exile, many Jews saw God's discipline as a chance for purification and responded with repentance. These formed a remnant that returned with a renewed heart for God.

In these last days, I believe there will be a similar remnant of those who fully embrace God's Word, living an authentic Christian life even in the face of persecution and increasing evil. This will serve as a testimony to others locally, nationally, and globally.

The Jews in Jesus's day also faced a similar situation, as illustrated in Matthew Chapter 13 where Jesus quoted Isaiah's prophecies and then continued his teaching by using parables. When the disciples asked why he spoke in parables, Jesus explained that understanding had not been granted to the people; it was too late for them. Yet not everyone misunderstood. Jesus said that God was concealing truth from the leaders and, with a hint of sarcasm, referred to them as the "wise and learned." This was God's way of hiding the truth from unreceptive people. Meanwhile, those with simple faith who took God's Word at face value had the truth revealed to them (Matthew 11:25-26).

Is this happening in churches today? The story of Noah and the Ark serves as another significant warning. Like the people in Noah's time, many today are preoccupied with life's pleasures and dismiss the prospect of judgment. Bible scholars estimate it took Noah 50 to 75 years to build the Ark, a timeline that mirrors the contemporary formation of signs of impending judgment. For instance, the establishment and ongoing prosperity of the State of Israel reflects this.

During Noah's decades-long work on the Ark, it likely served as a potent symbol to nearby residents. It is probable that Noah was frequently questioned about his construction project and may have faced ridicule for his efforts. Today, many groups and individuals are echoing warnings of impending judgment, and those who have been led astray may struggle to hear God's voice. I hope that despite all the noise being generated in society today, they hear clearly. To take advantage of the rescue being offered, you must distance yourself from the false teachings mentioned in this book and repent of any involvement.

Refusal to Believe Leads to Delusion

Failing to grasp Israel's role in God's plan results in significant short-sightedness, especially as we approach Jesus's return. He said we should watch for signs and one that consistently gets ignored in the New Churches and Western evangelical leadership is the return of the Jews to their homeland and the establishment of the State of Israel in 1948 – a glaringly obvious fulfilment of many Bible prophecies. This unmistakable sign demands attention, not only from the world but also from the Church.

Israel's resurrection and fulfilment of its prophetic destiny in alignment with God's Word present the last opportunity for nations and individuals to choose for or against the God of the Bible. When God's truth is plain, and you reject it, He allows delusion to set in. This not only entrenches unbelief but leads to acceptance of falsehoods (See Romans 1:18-28). The process described here in Romans 1 tells of the increase of God's wrath as He abandons them, "giving them over" to their false beliefs. This term refers to the handing over of a prisoner to receive their sentence. Urgent repentance is necessary to avoid being handed over to the delusions many parts of the church seem to prefer over the truth of His Word.

As throughout history, those who persistently reject the truth face judgment through the consequences of their actions. How far will God allow us to go before intervening? Accounts of the Flood, Sodom and Gomorrah, the Babylonian Captivity, and the Roman defeat of Israel in AD 70 emphasise God's patience and tolerance running out with dire consequences. Will the delusion afflicting the churches worsen due to their refusal to acknowledge the futility of their ideologies? Despite Restorationist or Kingdom Now beliefs, society isn't improving;

it's growing more perilous and hopeless. We're not progressing toward utopia, world peace, or prosperity. The planet and all creation groans under a curse, and despite our scientific, educational, technological, and material advancements, moral, spiritual, and social progress remains elusive. In some areas, we just become more comfortable and more entrenched in our misguided convictions.

You might disagree with this assessment, perhaps thinking that Jesus came to resolve the chaos, and now the Church has assumed that role. I must disagree; the world is unravelling just as Jesus predicted. If you think otherwise, you've been misled and need to return to His perspective on history. Things won't be restored until He returns. Believers must recognise that the Bible is God's revealed truth and align their thinking with it. A refusal to accept this gift of truth can lead to God permitting a strong delusion, resulting in poor choices and the embrace of increasingly bizarre and dangerous beliefs.

While God doesn't deceive people or tempt them with evil (James 1:13), He does allow those who do not love the truth to deceive themselves. If you've understood and accepted the concepts presented in this book, you should be contemplating your next steps.

Vandalism

The silence surrounding the issues I've raised in this book, especially regarding Israel, the Jews, deceptive theologies, and their connection to end-time signs, bewilders me. The teaching in some churches resembles a tapestry exhibited horizontally on a wall that you move along to view its unfolding story, like the Bayeux Tapestry, for example. The sad problem you encounter is that, as you move along to discover the Bible account, you find holes have been cut in it, or parts have been daubed with black paint. Sections of God's Big Story have been redacted, censored, or vandalised. But something even sadder accompanies this vandalism; very few people comment on the destruction. They don't ask about the missing parts.

Some churches do all the 'right things', good things: engaging in social action, establishing congregations, yet something feels amiss. I understand the adage 'you'll never find the perfect church,' and must acknowledge my own imperfections and need for repentance. I aim not to unfairly judge others, aware that my judgment reflects on me.

I do not want to unjustly criticise any church leader or genuine church stream. My goal is to shield believers from a growing threat to their security. Due to my past naivety, I may have led others astray. The Lord has forgiven me, and I have had to forgive myself. I now aim to change that. I don't want to regret, in a few years' time, that I should have done more.

Individual disciples undergo sanctification – a life of repentance, striving to grow closer to the Lord daily, discovering His mercies anew each morning. The collective life of believers should reflect this ongoing process too. To say, as a church leader once said to me, these issues are just a matter of opinion, is not good enough. Conflicting doctrines can't both be true, necessitating a pursuit of truth. Sadly, discussions questioning the status quo are absent or frowned upon.

In this day, with so many signs of the end appearing, it is sad that some churches do not want to bring up the issues related to Bible prophecy and therefore do not teach the whole word of God. This, as I have said, includes downgrading the Old Testament (see Rom 15:4 and 2 Tim 3: 14-17 which were written before the New Testament came together).

The End

In summarising this book, I must return to the key issue with which I began my journey of discovery: the undeniable connection between the future of the world and God's promises for Israel, Jerusalem, and the Jews. Commentators estimate that nearly 80% of the scriptures are devoted to Israel's origin, calling, chastisement, return to their land, and their future troubles–troubles that will soon engulf the entire world–and yet, some church leaders believe these parts of the Bible are not worthy of serious consideration.

When discussing the end times, the Old Testament prophets all begin with the same premise, and Jesus did likewise. Paul starts with Israel, Jerusalem, and the Jews when explaining how the world ends. Similarly, John, when writing of his God-given visions of the future in the Book of Revelation, also began with these crucial elements.

We aren't in the tribulation yet, but time is running out. We can already see the prophesied events beginning to unfold. While the complete fulfilment of these prophecies will occur during the seven-year tribulation, their shadows are evident now. We witness the establishment of a global economy, a global government, and a global religion, all in preparation for the antichrist's arrival.

People yearn for a strong leader who can bring peace and security to the world. Despite current appearances of stability, as societies crumble and the environment deteriorates, people will eagerly support anyone who can bring hope. Consent is being manufactured now, ready for his appearing.

And then there's the tribulation itself.

This period of world history is referred to variously as the Day of the Lord, the Tribulation—part of it, the Great Tribulation—and the time of Jacob's (Israel's) Trouble, or simply "that day." It will be a time of catastrophic judgments by God, on a scale never seen before or ever to be seen again, as Jeremiah prophesied:

How awful that day will be! No other will be like it. It will be a time of trouble for Jacob, but he will be saved out of it. (Jer. 30:7)

As believers, we must remain humble and avoid being dogmatic about our interpretations regarding the timing and manner of these events. Nevertheless, the Old Testament prophecies, Jesus' affirmations, his additions, and John's predictions in the Book of Revelation are clear: these events *will* happen.

Several specific wars are predicted in the scriptures around the start of the tribulation, and it's not clear which one triggers it. The conflict in Psalm 83 is seen by some scholars and commentators as a conglomeration of hostile nations symbolising all Israel's enemies throughout their history. Other Bible students note that none of these nations, or their modern counterparts, have ever joined forces to attack Israel together. Ten groups, which include Philistia (the land of the Philistines, now known as the Gaza), Tyre (now southern Lebanon), and Assyria (part of which is now Syria), surround and attack Israel.

Another war prophesied in Ezekiel 38 and 39 has different features: an attempted invasion from the north by nations corresponding to modern-day Iran and Russia.

As with many others, I believe God is in the process of fulfilling the prophecies of Zechariah 12:2-3:

I am going to make Jerusalem a cup that sends all the surrounding peoples reeling. Judah will be besieged as well as Jerusalem. On that day, when all the nations of the earth are gathered against her, I will make Jerusalem an immovable rock for all the nations. All who try to move it will injure themselves.

If this is the case, then we need to be open to hear what He is saying to us at this time. As the nations come against "Jerusalem," which in Zechariah 12 stands for all of Israel, we dare not pray against it, but we can continue to ask God to turn more Israelis into messianic believers who love their land and honour God's Word.

The church must be more knowledgeable about all of God's Word. With major prophetic events occurring more frequently and with increasing ferocity, the Body dare not be ignorant of the central place of Israel in what God is doing today. We know that God's Word includes all of the Tanach (the Jewish Scriptures) and the New Testament, but seemingly many born-again believers do not, or else they would be praying for and standing with Israel today.

When we read the Book of Revelation, we see the world at the point of no return as God's anger, held back for so long, is now poured out. Some examples of this follow: Chapter 6 describes judgments including the removal of peace from the earth, ensuing military conflicts, global economic collapse, rampant inflation and poverty, and the deaths of approximately two billion people from wars, famine, plague, and other perils.

The previous chapter sees Jesus unfurl a scroll by opening seals on it that each introduce a different phase of these judgments. There are seven seals, and upon the opening of the final seal in Chapter 8, seven trumpets herald further judgments. These include a massive earthquake, potentially triggering volcanic activity that ejects toxic dust and gases into the atmosphere. Hail and fire mixed with blood rain down upon the earth, followed by widespread bush and forest fires engulfing one-third of the planet. Subsequently, an asteroid, or something very similar, plummets to the earth causing one third of all the water sources on the planet to become contaminated.

Following the sounding of the seven trumpets, seven bowls containing God's wrath are poured out upon the earth, bringing further judgments faster and with more intensity.

While the Day of the Lord is a time of judgment, it also embodies remarkable grace and mercy. Chapter 7 of Revelation depicts the emergence of 144,000 Messianic believers (Jews who have embraced Christ) who evangelise both Jews and Gentiles during this tribulation period. In Chapter 14, God dispatches a powerful angel to proclaim the gospel worldwide. Through these actions and the escalating severity of the judgments, God endeavours to prompt humanity to repent.

As the pace and intensity of the judgments escalate, multitudes turn to God. Yet despite the unmistakable divine judgment, many refuse to repent (see Rev. 9:20-21, 16:9, and 16:11). This refusal is remarkably saddening.

At some point, either at the start of or early in the tribulation, Israel will be attacked by an overwhelming military force but, by divine intervention, they will escape complete destruction. This miracle leads all those left alive in Israel to turn to God and find Jesus. Another remarkable event then takes place: the hardening the Jews have experienced will be taken away and all

Israel will be saved, as stated in Romans 11:25-32.

Then the fulfilment of the prophetic scriptures of Isaiah 53 will come to pass. Here, Jews, at a future time—perhaps during Jesus's kingdom reign on earth—will look back and recount how their eyes were opened to see and understand the sacrifice of Jesus. They will tell how they had despised and rejected him, thinking he was stricken by God. Their salvation and revelation will enable them to see that it was because of their sin he died. As the veil dropped from their eyes, they recognised him as their Saviour and Messiah.

Declaring that all Bible prophecy has been fulfilled (as Fulfilment or Replacement Theology does) is indefensible and naïve, as we see many prophecies from the Old and New Testaments being realised today. To say that these prophecies somehow refer to the church is a nonsensical interpretation of these scriptures.

At the conclusion of the tribulation, Satan will be imprisoned for a thousand years while Jesus reigns with believers on earth. Given that the thousand-year period is reiterated six times in Chapter 20 of Revelation, it's remarkable that many church leaders deny its occurrence.

The references to these remarkable events and their global scale should alert us to the fact that we often view our faith from an individualistic perspective or accept the view of our church organisation or denomination. This is a part of Western culture that has infected the church.

Many church denominations, organisations and streams have been too inward-looking, failing to understand that a great drama and confrontation is being played out between the nations and the God who created them for His purpose—a confrontation that goes all the way back to the Tower of Babel. I hope that, in reading this book, you will experience something revelatory, insightful, and life changing.

We need to be impacted by global issues, such as the responsibility of nations for their sin against God and His laws, and the national responsibility and sin of Israel. As I reiterate

God's promises for Israel, I do not, at the same time, proclaim that Israel is deserving of them. On the contrary, many atrocities occur, some leaders conduct themselves lamentably in power, and not everything Israelis do is without fault or corruption. But if you're attacking Israel, you're essentially attacking God. They are still the apple of His eye, and He will restore them as He promised.

When I read the Bible, I notice that nations are spoken of only in terms of their relationship with God and Israel. For instance, the Psalms are full of references to the nations, the peoples, expressing the Psalmists' longing to see the nations praising God. In fact, the culmination of all salvation history is the victorious redemption of God, after millennia of struggles, finally affecting the nations.

The Day of the Lord, as spoken about by the Old Testament prophets, Jesus, and the Apostles, and as read in the Revelation of John, is a time when the rebellion of nations against God will be crushed, and they will acknowledge the people and nation God has chosen as the focal point of all nations.

As we read the Gospels, we see that Jesus's followers, steeped in the scriptures, fully expected him to establish an earthly kingdom and rule from Jerusalem (Acts 1:6).

During the millennium, Jesus *will* rule the nations from Jerusalem—and in a forceful way (Psalm 2:9; Revelation 12:5; Revelation 19:15). They will all be required to go up to Jerusalem to celebrate the Jewish Feast of Tabernacles, and any nation that does not go up will be punished (Zechariah 14:16-19). God's law and word will go out from Jerusalem. He will make judgements and settle disputes between nations, heralding an era of global peace (Isaiah 2:3-4; Micah 4:2; Zechariah 9:10).

We need to perceive the significance of events happening in the world today. God's regathering of His scattered people (Jeremiah 31:10) is a prelude to all Israel being saved and a precursor to the return of Jesus. Yet the church, which should be excited and supportive of this huge sign, is mostly silent and often blind to its prophetic meaning.

We have come to a time when enjoyable sermons full of undemanding life application lessons are past. We need sermons that contain the whole counsel of God to prepare us for the last days' realities, including the final rebellion of nations *against* God (2 Thessalonians 2:3) and the final judgement of nations *by* God.

Church leaders often avoid saying anything that might upset the status quo or make demands on believers. The unspoken mantra is "We've got to keep this thing going," fuelling the machinery behind the image of the popular church. Congregations have learned to accept what leaders say (or don't say) without question. They are happy to remain undisturbed by talk of the end times, yet they will listen to countless prophecies that remain unfulfilled.

Jeremiah confronted a similar situation in his day:

A horrible and shocking thing has happened in the land: the prophets prophesy lies, the priests rule by their own authority, and my people love it this way. But what will you do in the end? (Jeremiah 5:30-31).

The church is meant to make Jews envious by demonstrating a relationship with God that they, too, should be enjoying (Romans 10:19; 11:11). As Jews come to faith, they should unite with Gentiles, forming "one new man" (Ephesians 2:14-18). God intended this new humanity to challenge the principalities and powers of the air, but this has not occurred. Those who adhere to Replacement and Fulfilment Theology bear much of the responsibility for this failure.

Dear believer, can you now see the vast spiritual poverty that ravages the churches of the West—and now globally—because they are gripped by the false teachings warned against in this book?

Without the "one new man," the church cannot exhibit anything that will make Jews envious or oppose the plans of the principalities and powers ruling over the nations—not only rogue nations like Russia, China, North Korea, or Iran, but others as well.

If you want to understand any of the totalitarian regimes that operate around the world or understand what is happening in the Middle East, you must understand the forces driving them.

If you want to understand the increasing persecution of Jews (and Christians), you must understand its source. The Bible makes these things clear. As written earlier, the powers of darkness are always seeking to annihilate the Jews, especially now because their return to the land—although not yet fully complete—is well underway.

Once complete, it will set in motion terrible distress and anguish for them. This is the devastation by which that nation will be refined but then return as the redeemed of the Lord (Isaiah 35:10). They will then welcome their King, now contained in the heavens until the time comes for God to restore everything, as He promised long ago through His holy prophets (Acts 3:21).

This is the true restoration.

We are moving toward an ending where Israel and this genuine restoration—crucial to God's original objective for His creation—will become apparent. Many churches need to wake up to this reality.

Chapter 18

HOW SHOULD WE RESPOND?

Just Carry On?

What should we do next? One option is to do nothing, continuing in your current church situation, believing the issues raised in this book don't affect your church because it has the fundamentals right. However, it would be remiss of me to point out the errors without also discussing what needs to be done to free ourselves from the consequences of past mistakes. This chapter outlines some necessary actions.

Demolishing Strongholds

We must eliminate ungodly ideas that are strangling parts of the church, comprehensively refuting them with truth. We need to scrutinise the arguments behind this toxic mix and resist being fooled by the organisations that perpetuate them. We must avoid further generational loss by ceasing to pass on fabricated ideas that cause irreparable damage to the faith of younger believers. This legacy is poisoning them. We need to prevent the catastrophe that will cause vast numbers of people to fall away. All this must begin with repentance.

While distinguishing between the true 'ecclesia' of God and the man-made institutions we sometimes call 'churches', we see in the New Testament that the true 'ecclesia' can never come under condemnation. True believers undergo trials, but these are appointed for God's discipline so our faith can be refined. Provided we remain in Christ, we cannot come under His wrathful judgment because we are bound to Him in love. However, repentance is required to get back into the centre of His will.

Humility and repentance must be shown, beginning with leaders, then individual believers, whole local churches, and even church streams. Leaders should lead congregations in corporate repentance, recognising the errors discussed in this book. This may take time, but once done, a clear and emphatic distancing from false teaching, apologies, and a strong commitment to change and teach truth should follow. No more teaching Old Testament scripture as allegory; instead, believe and accept it as it is. There should be genuine efforts to undo the harm.

The doctrines of Replacement Theology, Restorationism, Kingdom Now theology, and any allegiance to the New Apostolic Reformation with its myriad deceptions should be renounced. Regret should be expressed over the degeneration of prophecy into a charismatic circus and the church's failure to be a true prophetic voice to the nation. Immoral laws passed while the church did nothing, and some parts became too focused on empire-building, should be acknowledged with sincere remorse.[1] Positive action demonstrating genuine repentance should be taken. Resources in the Appendix can help, especially if the issue of repentance or corporate repentance has never been discussed in your church.[2]

Where there have been dismissive or disparaging attitudes towards Jews and Jewish believers—including their predicament—a determined effort to support them should become evident. Acts of repentance by churches could be shown, for example, by helping Jews who reside in many parts of the world relocate to Israel. This is called "making Aliyah". Aliyah is not only a "Jewish" matter but mainly a "Kingdom of God" matter being fulfilled at this time. Several Christian charity organisations are currently endeavouring to do this, and churches could support them. There are strong biblical and prophetic links between Aliyah, Israel's salvation, and Jesus' return in glory.

Perhaps no issue in recent church history rivals the burden placed on leaders to now tell the truth. We've all done things in our lives we're not proud of, but we make amends by trying to make the future better for others. Without realising it, false teaching has significantly impacted the lives of thousands of believers and has a direct correlation to the spiritual health of individuals, churches, and church streams.

Church leaders, having read the claims of this book, now have the opportunity to put things right and help current and future believers avoid the problems others are facing – and will face if there is no change.

If You Have Ears to Hear

If you grasp this book's message but your leaders show no comprehension or desire to repent over these issues, then gather with like-minded believers to form small groups. You will have to face the question of whether to leave your church or stay in the hope of being an agent of change. Pray fervently for your church or fellowship's understanding of these matters and seek the Lord's guidance while studying His Word. Make use of the reference material provided. Don't let information and misinformation overwhelm you to the point of giving up on truth. Commit it to God, asking for His help, and draw close to Him.

No Retreat

Although I write a lot about hard times ahead, this book is not a call to retreat. We still have a commission to preach the Gospel and lead others to salvation.

When the people of God were taken captive into Babylon they were told to get involved in the affairs of that nation seek its prosperity and pray for it. To do all this and effectively reach out, we must be built up, confident in our faith, knowledgeable about the Word, and aware of our place in God's plan.

Do not neglect personal devotion to the Word of God and prayer. In these challenging days, take personal responsibility to seek the Lord, read your Bible, pray, and seek His face. Strengthen and build yourself up in your most holy faith.

Additionally, there is a corporate aspect. Meeting in large groups may become difficult, but forming small home groups to study God's Word and pray together can provide mutual encouragement and strength among believers. Now, more than ever, the remnant of Bible-believing disciples should engage in this practice.

The end of all things is near. Therefore, be alert and of sober mind so that you may pray. (1 Peter 4:7).

The Greek word used here for "end" is never used in the New Testament as a chronological end, as if something simply stops. Instead, the word means a consummation, a goal achieved, a result attained, or a realisation. Peter is emphasising the second coming of Christ, which is the goal of all things. He is calling believers to live obediently and expectantly in the light of Christ's return.

When he exhorts us to "be alert and of sober mind," he means that we should not be swept away by emotions or passions, thus maintaining a proper eternal perspective on life. When he says the time is near, he means imminent; that is, the return of Jesus Christ could be at any moment. The doctrine of the imminent return of Christ should not turn the Christian into a zealous fanatic who does nothing but wait for it to occur. Instead, it should motivate believers to share the Gospel, warn others, and pursue holiness.

As believers, we should always be looking to purify ourselves, but the Bible suggests we will do it more intentionally and with greater enthusiasm when our thoughts are fixed on Christ's soon return (1 John 3:3). In his description of the terrors of end-time events and amid exhortations to not be afraid (see Luke 21), Jesus said we should look up. The arrival of things that mark the last days should be a cause of great expectation, joy, and triumph for the believer.

When these things begin to take place, stand up and lift up your heads, because your redemption is drawing near. (Luke 21:28).

If these remarkable things are never mentioned in your

church, you are unlikely to want to clean up your act. Do you have a proper eternal perspective on life, or has this been dulled by the false idea that Christ will not return until the church makes the world ready for Him?

(Incidentally, you may notice that I have not mentioned the belief held by some Christians regarding the snatching away of believers to heaven before the Tribulation. To adequately address this event, often referred to as "The Rapture," I would need to study it thoroughly to provide a comprehensive and accurate account, as I have done with the other topics discussed so far. Covering this topic in detail would require another book! For now, I have included some notes on this subject in the Appendix).

We need to fellowship together with the aim of praying about all these things, studying what the Bible says about them, and helping others to discover them.

And let us consider how we may spur one another on towards love and good deeds, not giving up meeting together, as some are in the habit of doing, but encouraging one another – and all the more as you see the Day approaching.
(Hebrews 10:24-25).

If you've left a local church and aren't yet in fellowship with other believers, prioritise finding Christians in your local area for small group fellowship. There is some material in the Appendix to help with this.

The tide has turned but many have not realised and are still playing on the sandbank. Be aware of this. Get off the sandbank of false beliefs and onto the firm foundation of God's Word.

Notes:
[1] See links to the leaflet about Ungodly Laws in the Appendix
[2] See links to the leaflet about Repentance and Intercession in the Appendix

EPILOGUE

Global Changes

Since I started writing and up to the publication date, several world-altering events have occurred. No one foresaw the 2019 Covid outbreak in China, which evolved into a global pandemic. Nor did anyone expect to see the West at war with Russia in the 2020s.

While these events may seem devastating, from a global and historical perspective, I choose to see them as acts of God's grace and mercy. The spread of Covid-19 highlighted the possibility of a global pandemic, a concept previously overlooked by today's generation. Similarly, the threat of nuclear war or a nuclear disaster, largely dismissed until now, has come closer to reality with Vladimir Putin's leadership.

With the rise of the Black Lives Matter movement, another aspect of Cultural Marxism's driving force, Critical Theory, emerged: Critical Race Theory. This rebellious ideology aims to remove law and order controls with its calls to defund the police. Don't be shocked by these developments; they are signs of the times (see 2 Thess. 2:3).

Totalitarianism, traditionally associated with China, North Korea, and Russia, became evident in Western countries as some governments exploited the Covid-19 crisis to exert unnecessary control.

The frequency of natural disasters also increased. To this list of changes, we can add potential global financial collapse, the effects of what is called climate change, and wildlife extinction often through man-made pollution, all worsening since I began this book.

God didn't create these events, but He is using them to show that things prophesied in the Bible can now easily occur. They've always happened but are becoming more frequent and intense as history nears its end.

For churches and leaders who have not brought the matters of the end times to the attention of their congregations, God intends for you to take notice.

Closer to Home

In UK churches, leaders proposed and conducted same-sex weddings and blessing services affirming ungodly lifestyles and practices. While we should reach out to and welcome these groups and individuals, we cannot condone sin. It's challenging to distinguish between churches genuinely reaching out and those diluting the Gospel to stay relevant in changing times – a drift that can affect entire denominations or church streams.

The prediction from the "prophet" in June 2018[1] about blessings for my local church over a three-year period didn't come true (see section entitled 'Under an Illusion' in Chapter 13). I felt sad for this person and the churches affected by this and other messages he must have given out. I prayed he would get help with this matter but, more importantly, that an explanation would be given to the churches in which he spoke.

Incidentally, none of the "prophets" in the New Churches or in any of the churches and ministries of the NAR foresaw the advent of the Coronavirus yet they often claimed to be hearing from God. And most of these prophets predicted that President Trump would get re-elected to a 2nd term. Are these the kind of prophecies that God condemned in Jeremiah's day? (see Jer. 14:13-15 and 23:20-22).

In the years since I embarked on this journey of discovery, the issues I aimed to alert the church to have worsened considerably. I have often had to use terms such as 'false teaching' and 'deception'. This can sound very negative, but I am simply attempting to identify errors so that we can recognise them and repent where necessary.

The attention I have had to give to these negative aspects has saddened me, but I will not apologise for writing this book. These things needed to be said. As my investigations continued, I became increasingly concerned about church leaders either being silent about important issues or tampering with scripture, making it say what they wanted rather than what God intended – and doing it all without fear!

In these days of social fragmentation and collapse, cultural accommodation, and the growing threat of war, the message remains that God can still save us. Even at this late hour, when judgement seems unavoidable, God wants to have mercy. All we need to do is repent.

Notes:
[1] Approximately 18 months after this prophecy the first cases of the Coronavirus were reported in the UK and soon after we started to go into lockdown. In June 2021 (three years after the prophecy) MPs were still debating when to end Covid-19 restrictions. See BFPG Covid-19 Timeline at: https://bfpg.co.uk/2020/04/covid-19-timeline

Appendix 1

THE NEW AGE MOVEMENT

Ambiguity

The term "New Age" is notoriously ambiguous, used by some people working towards a new world order but not universally adopted. Some openly identify as New Agers, while others prefer terms like Alternative Spirituality. I'll use the catch-all term 'New Age Movement' to refer to all these groups.

Before my conversion, I encountered the movement in the '60s and '70s, thinking it was confined to small fringe groups. It may have been then, but things have evolved.

My initial research, including simplified work like Wikipedia, was a starting point. However, if you research these issues, it's crucial not to stop there—verify information through other sources.

A word of caution: approaching original, foundational books on this subject requires preparation and prayer. I relied on research by Dr. Clifford Denton, who spent two years studying the New Age Movement, resulting in a booklet series titled *"The Christian Response to the New Age Movement."*

Dr. Denton highlights the deceitfulness of the present time, echoing Jesus' warning about deception in Matthew 24. He describes groups within the movement and their expectations:

... groups of people who are expecting a new era to emerge for mankind, an era in which solutions will be found to many global problems, an age of release of spiritual awareness and

harmony on this planet, an age of expectancy for a new world order and leadership. It includes people who are working for some or part of that global plan, or are applying some or all of the teaching to their lives that can be linked, in some way, to this thinking.

Jesus said, 'My Kingdom is not of this world' (John 18:36), and the Bible records many signs of the end of this age so, though Christians expect Jesus to return, the manner of His coming, the reason for his coming and the expectations surrounding his coming are different from those with a philosophy for a New Age dawning on this earth. Thus, we do not include Christians as New-Agers, even though the counterfeit that is contained in much of New Age thinking seems very similar to Christian teaching.[1]

All the major crises that the world is facing today, including political upheaval, climate change, finance, sociology, education, and global health have groups of people busying themselves trying to find solutions. They are global problems, and many people are looking for ways to understand and solve them.

Dr. Denton outlines how those involved are vulnerable to acting without due care:

The concerns are often good ones and rightly motivated. However, there is a doorway to deception when a wrong understanding about God and how he is to be found becomes a part of the solution to the problems. In desperation, or for pride or personal gain, men will believe a lie and go down a road of terrible deception, leading others behind them. This is the danger of the New Age Movement and organisations which are influenced by them.[2]

This applies to church leaders, churches, and church streams too.

A new wave of spiritual seeking is gaining popularity. It features an openness to experience and experimentation. For instance, we know that the Bible says that there is some value in keeping our bodies healthy (see 1 Tim 4:8), but when we see people attempting to channel healing energies from the universe's store of power, or engaging in spiritual meditation that is not Bible-based, we must conclude that people are opening their lives to demonic powers. Furthermore, caring for wildlife and the natural habitats of various creatures, although good motivations in themselves, have led, in many places, to the worship of Mother Earth. If we see this happening, we must conclude that deception has come in.

Dr. Denton comments on the trend to experiment and points out its links:

This experimentation has brought in a fascination with the mystical religions of the East, particularly Hinduism, but also other ancient religions. People are opening themselves to various combinations of teaching from these religions. As people derive their own concept of who or what God is, outside of Christ, seeking spiritual powers to help them solve their problems, we can say that a massive deception is about to be launched on humanity.[3]

Most New Agers talk and write about 'transformation,' and this is desired on two levels. The first transformation is a personal one whereby a human being recognises his or her oneness with all things in the universe. The second transformation being sought is a planetary one. This takes place when a critical mass of human beings reaches this same awareness. This is also seen as initiation. It is believed, in New Age circles, that we are currently undergoing this transformation – or transition – into a New Age, with a new consciousness.

Even some brief investigations of the movement reveal the individual and small group adherence to these beliefs, but the global connections to them are staggering. Many people worldwide are seeking global cooperation to solve global problems and are turning to the teachings of many contemporary proponents of the movement, as well as the long-established ones such as Helena Blavatsky and Alice Bailey.

Alice in Wonderland

In one of the booklets in Dr. Denton's New Age series he

focuses on the works of Alice Bailey, who should be regarded as a founder member of the movement. During a thirty-year period in the early 1900s, Alice A. Bailey, in "telepathic collaboration" with the Tibetan teacher she called Djwhal Khul, wrote two dozen volumes on what she said were the origins and evolutionary development of Matter and Consciousness within our solar system, our planet, and human society.

Her writings tried to describe the forces and energies in the universe and beyond, which, she said, can be consciously developed, controlled, and directed. Based on the "ageless wisdom" of the world's religious traditions, yet updated for the needs of our modern intelligence, these teachings attempted to reveal a path to what she called soul consciousness and the establishment of right human relations. She was one of the first writers to use the term 'New Age.'

Bailey was influenced by Helena Blavatsky, another founder of the New Age movement, when she became involved in the Theosophical Society in the US following her move to America and the start of her writing in 1922. She disagreed with the Theosophical Society over various issues and was eventually dismissed by them. She then founded the Lucifer Trust, later renamed the Lucis Trust, and continued her prolific writing career. Alice Bailey's writings appear to comprise a plan that is revealed in a set of books and booklets, the intention of which was to liberate the world from the restrictions and yokes of traditional Christianity and look for the coming of a New Age in which sexual freedom, abortion, homosexuality, and the destruction of the family would all feature strongly.

She was a powerful occultist who had spiritual masters controlling her. Her autobiography states that at the age of fifteen she had an unusual experience that was to affect her for the rest of her life. Dr. Denton again:

While alone in her home one Sunday a man in European clothes and wearing a turban walked into the room and talked with her. He told her that she could have an important role in the world providing she could change her character suitably. If she were willing then he would be in touch with her over the coming years and that she would travel the world 'doing her masters work'.[4]

Bailey claimed that most of her writings were "received" from the Tibetan teacher.

There is a great deal of Hindu and Buddhist thought running through these works, even though they have been adapted to suit the rational western mind. Although rooted in eastern thought, the ideas can be shaped and adapted into contemporary scientific and philosophical thought as if to bring into being an attractive, new form of religious knowledge.

Dr. Denton comments on the pervasive nature of this:

Through the Arcane School, World Goodwill, The Lucis Trust, The Theosophical Society, The New Group of World Servers, and other schools of esoteric and occult teaching of New Age ideas, the works of Alice Bailey are increasingly promoted. As we have pointed out in earlier briefing papers these groups are becoming very influential and have even drawn in members of bodies such as the United Nations as well as other eminent people in a variety of fields of operation. Alice Bailey said of herself over 50 years ago:

"I became next an occult student, a writer of books which have had a wide and constant circulation and which have been translated into many languages. I found myself at the head of an esoteric school - all unwittingly and without any planned intention - and the organiser, with Foster Bailey, of an international Goodwill Movement (not a peace movement) which proved so successful that we had centres in nineteen countries when the war broke out in 1939."[5]

Reaching New Generations

The idea of a New Group of World Servers has been embraced by subsequent individuals and groups who have been taken in by notions of helping to create a better world through various programs of group consciousness – 'tuning in to the vibrations' of others.

In an overview of the movement, Dr Denton explains how Alice Bailey 'prophesied' that the New Age movement would start as an underground one but emerge to coincide with the Age of Aquarius. It would be a cooperative effort, which many organisations now consider as appropriate to their participation, not as one big, organised body but various parts acting together behind the scenes. It bears many similarities to the networking patterns found when church streams, para-church organisations and ministries work together. This is where discernment is needed.

Anyone who was born in my era – the 1950s, 60s or even later, in the 70s – might now be a patriarch or matriarch in the media, education, business, national government or other important area. Many of these may have been influenced through Bailey's writings. Throughout the 70s, 80s and 90s, potential influencers were themselves being influenced and finding strategic positions in the world. Some of these are likely to have become policy makers in the United Nations, the World Health Organisation, the International Monetary Fund, the Hollywood film industry, the World Economic Forum, the World Bank, or other powerful global organisations.

A major part of Bailey's long-term strategy was to avoid trying to change the minds of adults. She suggested that young people should be targeted – especially the more educated. She proposed that by working this way, every generation that followed would be more receptive to the plan than the previous one. Eventually, the components of the plan would become such a normal part of life because mindsets would have been created to accommodate its implementation.

Influencing younger generations in the Arts and media was part of this plan. She wanted to see the Arts run wild. She succeeded in this; many of the artists we associate with the modern art movements in the US followed the teachings of Theosophy with its connections to eastern religions.

Another of her aims, following any subversions implemented in society, was to get the Church to surrender ground and officially support them.

Incidentally, you might not be surprised to learn that her writings, so obviously demonic, include a heavy dose of antisemitism.

It would have been beyond belief to the people of the 1920s and 30s that the things being proposed then would actually come to pass but, as you see, these things have happened and are happening.

The fact that the aims of Alice Bailey and those like her have succeeded helps you see that the spiritual forces behind her have been very active. The enemy has been moving up the gears because he knows his time is short.

I must warn you again that although all of Bailey's books are readily available through the usual sources, I would not recommend that you read and study them directly. There are other sources, written by believers who have studied them and have reported on them. Do not do it unless, first, you have a thorough knowledge of scripture and, second, that you are fully prepared by being covered in your own protective prayers and those of a group of intercessors. There is a lot of very dark and influential material here. This is spiritual warfare, so don't take on battles for which you are not equipped.

The Age of Aquarius

Another book, of major influence, that has been dubbed "a Blueprint for the New Age Movement",[6] gives an indispensable understanding of the movement. It is *The Aquarian Conspiracy* by Marylin Ferguson, who is herself a New-Ager.

Ferguson uses the term "conspiracy" in the old-fashioned sense of a group of people working and co-operating together to a common end and benign purpose. She posited that other groups should be developed and networked and that each network should represent a part of the whole change that was being ushered in. This now global network *is* the Aquarian Conspiracy, which seeks to inspire new ways of thinking in all areas of society: science, government, medicine, education, law, art, psychology, and religion.

Dr. Denton comments on the book:

To read the book The Aquarian Conspiracy is, in itself, a battle against a major seduction that tells you to let go of the things that chain you down and jump out in exploration of new ideas and experience. For people who are lost and seeking solutions to life's problems, this is a compelling idea. It becomes the doorway for any and every exploration. No doubt some explorations will create solutions. However, this new philosophy allows anything to be a reasonable route for exploration. It discounts nothing as invalid in the route to personal transformation.[7]

Dr. Denton points out the dangerous omission: that, because of the fall, man is totally depraved, cannot save himself and needs a saviour. The New-Ager will say that you should experiment and explore to find the latent god within. You should discover the god who is part of everything and, through this, connect with the powers and energies of the universe.

He reveals more:

It is a massive lie that gives plausibility to Eastern religions, particularly Hinduism. It gives an open door to experimentation with drugs, with transcendental meditation, to magic, to astrology. The unknown becomes a mystery to be discovered. The individual will make his or her transformation by experimenting in many of the areas where conventional thinking has put up barriers.[8]

The Aquarian Conspiracy is another publication that, like Bailey's books, I was wary of studying personally. So, I was grateful to Dr Denton for his work.

Hidden Dangers

I was also grateful for the work of Christian lawyer Constance Cumbey in *The Hidden Dangers of the Rainbow*.[9] I found her book to be a valuable source of information and insight. Cumbey delves into aspects of New Age movements, such as the anticipated arrival of Lord Maitreya, a figure awaited by New Agers who, as part of a New World Order, will bring about global peace, redistribute world assets, reorganise political systems, and establish a one-world religion.

She draws our attention to a global media campaign launched in 1982, in which a press advertisement displayed the heading *'Who is the Christ?'* and gave this explanation:

Throughout history, humanity's evolution has been guided by a group of enlightened men, the Masters of Wisdom. They have remained largely in the remote desert and mountain places of earth, working mainly through their disciples who live openly in the world. This message of the Christ's reappearance, has been given primarily by such a disciple trained for his task for over 20 years. At the centre of this "Spiritual Hierarchy" stands the World Teacher, LORD MAITREYA, known by Christians as the CHRIST. And as Christians await the Second Coming, so the Jews await the MESSIAH, the Buddhists the FIFTH BUDDHA, the Moslems the IMAM MAHDI, and the Hindus await KRISHNA. These are all names for one individual. His presence in the world guarantees there will be no third World War.

Many Bible scholars see this character as being the prophesied antichrist. In the era of the New Testament church, the believers thought that, because he persecuted them so cruelly, the Roman Emperor Nero was the antichrist, and during the Second World War, Hitler appeared to be the perfect match. There have been many antichrists throughout the centuries and, no doubt, the devil has always had someone waiting in the wings to achieve his aims, but the time is approaching when we will see the ultimate fulfilment of this prophecy.

Despite unfulfilled predictions of his arrival around the time of the press campaign, he is still eagerly awaited. We know from the Bible who he really is and that he must appear soon. Most churches in the West will not teach correctly, if they teach at all, on eschatological issues. Leaders of my New Church stream teach that this character has already been on earth and done his worst.[10]

Prophecies in both the Old Testament and in the New

often have more than one fulfilment so we need to be careful not to dismiss a possible later one simply because we think the prophecy has been realised.

New Church leaders also dismiss end-time prophecies about the Tribulation for example because they believe the church will bring heaven on earth and don't want to consider anything that might prevent this.

Cumbey comments on this blinkered view:

The biblical warnings are also clear that the final beast of the world would be diverse from the others and trample the entire world underfoot, horribly persecuting the saints in the process. Its coming may be inevitable. Nevertheless, it should not be established on the backs of naive Christians who are more taken by deceptive New Age promises than with clear scriptural warnings.[11]

Cumbey also points out the similarities between New Age beliefs and those enshrined in Humanism. Most churches in the West, if they ever mention these issues, will include warnings about not being influenced by conspiracy theories. Along with the New-Agers and the Humanists they say that there is no evidence to show that there is some kind of plot to take over the world, but Cumbey argues that, on the contrary, there is:

The Humanist Manifesto[12] *affirms: that the universe created itself; that promises of salvation are harmful; that ethics are situational; that individuals should have the right to abortion and should have total sexual freedom; and that socialism should be in control worldwide.*

And goes on to say:

These are the exact beliefs with which our children are brainwashed in public schools beginning in kindergarten. They are predominant today in our universities and in government. And these very same beliefs are being promoted cleverly and persistently by the national news media.[13]

A Contemporary Movement

As mentioned earlier in this chapter, the movement is not to be viewed as simply the ideas of a bunch of oddballs who babbled their way through the 60s and 70s.

As part of my research, I utilised the website https://www. academia.edu, a platform where academics share research papers. The site boasts that millions of academics use Academia. edu to share their research, monitor the impact of their research, and track the research of academics they follow. Over 127 million have signed up, and it attracts over 64 million unique visitors a month.

The site allows you to download papers such as PhD dissertations in any field of academic study. Being curious to see if the New Age movement would be regarded as a credible and worthy subject to study among our up-and-coming scholars, I was surprised to find that there were thousands of papers being submitted on this and similar topics supporting New Age and New Thought ideas.

Alongside papers on, for example, politics, history, and the sciences, one young academic submitted *The Esoteric Philosophy of Alice A. Bailey: Ageless Wisdom for a New Age*[14] in which he defends Bailey's writings against *'traditional assumptions'* he regards as *'unwarranted in light of our modern understanding'*.

Many New-Agers, even though they may not refer to themselves as such, are currently in places of influence. The position of these people may range between an official in global governance to a teacher at your local school to an administrator on your local church staff team.

Some churchgoers mix New Age and New Thought with the Bible to create progressive belief systems they believe are Christian.

The hugely successful TV host, media producer and executive, actress and author, Oprah Winfrey, is very vocal in espousing and expressing New Age thought and beliefs.

In 2007 she began to endorse the self-help program *The Secret* which employs the use of the pseudoscientific technique called the power or Law of Attraction.[15] This 'Law' asserts that people can change their lives for the better through positive thoughts or 'vibrations'.

In 2008 Winfrey publicised the overtly New-Age book *A New Earth: Awakening to Your Life's Purpose* by Eckhart Tolle through her TV book club. During a Webinar class, in which she promoted the book, she is quoted as saying "God is a feeling experience and not a believing experience. If your religion is a believing experience ... then that's not truly God."[16]

Other New Age thinking you may find in your church includes the maintaining of a false unity, a oneness with others where any kind of disagreement is seen as a disruption of spiritual harmony. Here you must not challenge anyone's beliefs as being wrong. Avoiding petty conflicts is essential, but when unity becomes an idol, it displaces the Gospel and allows false teaching to take root.

Pluralism is another threat whereby a mixing together of Christian beliefs with the more recognised and tolerated cultural beliefs in society make your message more acceptable. Some churches want people to become Christians without giving them the Christian message because they don't want to offend anyone.

Universalism, another New Age belief, has a grip in many churches. In this view, all people get saved in the end, regardless of their beliefs. This creates a powerful disincentive to evangelise. There is no wrath in this view of God because he is all love. I believe this error creeps into the church firstly through the downgrading of Old Testament scriptures and a re-telling of God's Big Story that leaves out our Hebraic roots. Through this, people start to doubt the truth of the creation story, the flood, Sodom and Gomorrah, the Covenants, and other accounts of God's dealings with humans.

Finally, various types of mysticism have been adopted by some Christians and, although we don't want to invalidate genuine seeking after God and searching the Scriptures to discover deep truths, it's essential to approach it from a secure place. Mysticism features in many religions but we need to be aware of how it infiltrates the Christian experience. I recommend another booklet in the series by Dr Clifford Denton previously mentioned which concentrates on this subject.[17]

Dr Denton gives an excellent overview of this topic. He discusses early proponents of mysticism, and more recent adherents such as Ravi Ravindra and Matthew Fox.

Same Symbol, Different Promise

Considering that I have referenced a book claiming there are dangers connected to the rainbow emblem, it would be remiss of me in closing this report not to mention the use – or misuse – of that symbol and its alignment with New Age thinking. Many organisations from the multi-nationals, to non-profits, to global corporations, to UN organisations, several global charities, environmental groups, retail outlets, and now, TV advertisements display the rainbow symbol in some form or other.

The most recognisable use, of course, is by the LGBTQ+ movement.

Since Constance Cumbey's book was published in 1983, all the things she wrote about have become more prevalent. Tolerance toward the LGBTQ+ ideology, birthed in the sexual revolution of the 50s and 60s, is not agreed with by many people in the UK but dissenters cannot be listened to and must be dismissed as bigots and "haters". Although the mantra 'unity with diversity', coined by Alice Bailey, sounds good, it is in practice extremely exclusionary and often discriminates against Christians.

In the same way that the red flags and banners proliferated in the soviet bloc years ago, so the rainbow flags in the West now signal a similar set of lies. Then it was the upholding of the myth that a socialist society was great and good and the best way to live – even in the face of government repression, imprisonment, and torture for those who disagreed.

Now, the rainbow flags challenge you to disapprove of the ideology they proclaim and those who do so privately must be careful never to speak publicly about what they secretly think. Torture may not follow, but losing one's job and income might be akin to imprisonment and torture for some. The time is here when Christians will be expected to conform and, if they don't, they will be shamed. After that, if they still don't conform, they will be persecuted.

A Summary of This Research

If you were born in the last 20, 30 or even 40 years, you need to know it wasn't always like this. There was a time when most of the population in the West believed in God. Even if they weren't all born-again believers, many people went to church. There was an underlying fear of God and a desire to 'do the right thing'.

In the 1960s and 70s I saw the greatest changes in Western society and a time when the UK lost its belief in God. The problem is, as G. K. Chesterton said, when you stop believing in God you don't then believe in nothing - you believe in anything!

I do not want you to become anxious or fearful. If you are a true believer, then be assured that God is watching over you. If there is anything that has worried you in what I have written, then take it to God in prayer and cast all your cares on him. He cares for you.

Try to discover for yourself about the things written of here. Maybe do a Bible study on end-time events. Check the references and links I have given to help you do this and earnestly seek God for truth. Despite the troubling times, by getting close to him you can know a peace that only he can give.

Notes:

[1] Denton, C. (1990), *The Challenge of the New Age Movement*, London, PWM Trust, p3

[2] Ibid, p4

[3] Ibid, p4

[4] Denton, C. (1990), *Foundations of New Age Thinking: The Works of Alice Bailey*, London, PWM Trust, p3.

[5] Ibid, p4

[6] Denton, C. (1990), *The Challenge of the New Age Movement*, London, PWM Trust, p5

[7] Ibid, p5.

[8] Ibid, p6

[9] Cumbey, C. (1983), *The Hidden Dangers of the Rainbow*, Huntingdon House Inc., Lafayette, LA p14.

[10] The then leader of New Frontiers, teaching in a public meeting in 2017, as part of a series on the book of Daniel, said that the Abomination of Desolation, perpetrated by the anti-Christ, described in Chapter 9, happened in AD 70. This, and all other prophecies like it, have all been fulfilled according to the Fulfillment Theology view.

[11] Ibid, p158.

[12] Note: *The Humanist Manifesto* of 1933 (which has been superseded by more recent declarations of a very similar nature) is a basically a statement that many academics, lawyers, writers, theologians and church leaders, sociologists, and philosophers signed-up to and agreed with. It declared in essence that we can build a much better world without God and conventional religion. Search online: *The Humanist Manifesto*.

[13] Ibid, p153.

[14] Borsos, D. (2012), *The Esoteric Philosophy of Alice A. Bailey: Ageless Wisdom for a New Age*, A Dissertation submitted to the Faculty of the California Institute of Integral Studies in Partial Fulfilment of the Requirements for the Degree of Doctor of Philosophy in Integral Studies with a concentration in Learning and Change in Human Systems, San Francisco, CA

[15] Alice Bailey wrote much about a Hierarchy of beings (Buddha and Christ being two) bringing the New Age to humankind by methods such as the imparting of 'Secrets'. See Denton, C. (1990), *Foundations of New Age Thinking: The Works of Alice Bailey*, London, PWM Trust, pages 12 and 17.

[16] See the US online magazine, *The Christian Post*, April 2008, (last accessed 06.08.21) at https://www.christianpost.com or search: Oprah Winfrey Eckhart Tolle.

[17] Denton, C. (1991), *Truth About Deception in the Present Age: Mysticism*, London, PWM Trust

Appendix 2

CULTURAL MARXISM

Another Conspiracy Theory?

If you research Cultural Marxism, you will face assertions that it does not exist and is a conspiracy theory.

Steve Maltz, who has written extensively on this subject, claims that there used to be a Wikipedia page entitled Cultural Marxism but if you search for it now, you will be taken to a section on the pages about the Frankfurt School – where this ideology came from – entitled *Cultural Marxism conspiracy theory*.

Wikipedia, who loudly declare their neutrality, appear to have already decided anyone who believes that Cultural Marxism exists is deluded.

Maltz describes a dilemma in which two entirely different views about the aims of this institution are present in society. I checked out Wikipedia's view:

The Frankfurt School (Frankfurter Schule) is a school of social theory and critical philosophy associated with the Institute for Social Research, at Goethe University Frankfurt. Founded in the Weimar Republic (1918-33), during the European interwar period (1918-39), the Frankfurt School comprised intellectuals, academics, and political dissidents who were ill-fitted to the contemporary socio-economic systems (capitalist, fascist, communist) of that time. The Frankfurt School proposed that social theory was inadequate for explaining the turbulent factionalism and reactionary politics of capitalist societies in the

20th century. Critical of capitalism and Marxism-Leninism as philosophically inflexible systems, the School's Critical Theory research indicated alternative paths to realising the social development of a society and a nation.[1]

Here is the problem: is this simply an agreeable bunch of experts giving helpful advice or are they the instigators of, not just theoretical ideas, but a plan of action – a long march – to implement its objectives over a prolonged period?

Maltz clarifies it by saying he subscribes to the more threatening view because he believes that it is where the evidence leads. He continues:

The main reason why many cannot bring themselves to agree with this view is that it reads like a plot of a Dan Brown or Frederick Forsyth novel. I have to admit that the conclusions derived from the clear evidence seem to be downright unbelievable. But that doesn't make it untrue.[2]

What is this evidence Maltz speaks of?

I have had personal experience of this brand of Marxism operating in our culture and you have too, although you may not have realised it. I have also studied it to a point where I can say that there is indisputable evidence that it does exist and that it is the root cause of many of the socio-political problems in the Western world.

Before we delve deeper, we must acknowledge a significant hurdle obstructing a clear understanding of its true nature – the opposition it faces from the far-right. This often takes an extreme form because most of the main characters in this story are Jewish. This has led to claims of a Jewish conspiracy. It isn't, but you can almost excuse others for thinking it. While it is true that Karl Marx and key members of the Frankfurt School were of Jewish descent, this does not substantiate the claims. The individuals who continue to promote these ideas today, whether activists or theoreticians, may have Jewish backgrounds, but this in no way validates the notion of a coordinated Jewish conspiracy.

Leaving that aside, let's go on to discover how this neo-Marxism influenced Western culture.

Reconfiguring the Lie

You're likely familiar with the birth of Marxism and the communist ideology in the mid-1800s. Karl Marx, the progenitor of these ideas, primarily focused on economic theories. He advocated for the working classes to rise up and establish a fairer society through wealth redistribution, often promoting the necessity of a revolution. He passionately wrote and lectured, hoping to see his vision realised. It eventually materialised in Russia in 1917, though Marx himself didn't live to witness it. His ideas, rooted in atheism and humanism, resonated with others who believed in their potential. They used his writings as a foundation, expanding and modifying them to call for revolutions across the Western world.

When the First World War erupted, these communists saw it as a pivotal moment. They envisioned the working classes of different nations coming together in an international brotherhood, choosing not to engage in war but instead to revolt against the ruling classes. However, this intention clashed with remnants of Christian values and patriotism within the population. Instead of rebelling, the working classes enlisted to fight for their respective countries, deeply disappointing the Marxists.

This turn of events raises questions about the true motives of the Marxists. Did they genuinely seek the best for the working classes? Or was it ideology for the sake of ideology? When combined with an atheistic and humanistic foundation, the answer appears clear: Rebellion.

Rebellion forms the core and purpose of Marxism.

Following the failure of several revolutions, a group of German Marxist intellectuals and academics based at the Institute for Marxism in Frankfurt, later renamed the Institute for Social Research (ISR), felt compelled to address the shortcomings of 19th-century classical Marxism. They believed it couldn't adequately address the social issues of the 20th century.

The scholars at the Institute, commonly referred to as the Frankfurt School, embarked on redefining Marxism. They shifted its focus from economics to the culture that enveloped society as a whole. In 1923, Felix Weil, a wealthy Jewish entrepreneur, established, funded, and staffed the school. Their primary objective was to reorganise Classical Marxism to address culture, achieved through the creation and development of a social theory for change, which they termed Critical Theory

Critical Theory

Critical Theory, often seen as complex and mysterious, has a core philosophy: a set of neo-Marxist techniques designed to dismantle established structures. It lacks positivity, identifying valid concerns in Western society but offering no solutions, only urging rebellion.

Essentially, Critical Theory embodies destructive criticism of key facets of Western culture, including Christianity, capitalism, authority, the family, patriarchy, hierarchy, morality, tradition, sexual restraint, loyalty, patriotism, nationalism, convention, and conservatism.

In his insightful book on the subject, Melvin Tinker explains the raison d'être:

In 1930 Max Horkheimer became the director of the ISR which is when neo-Marxism was launched in earnest. Horkheimer was convinced that the major obstacle to the spread of Marxism was traditional Western culture with its Judeo-Christian heritage. Here there developed a revisionist neo-Marxist interpretation of Western culture under the rubric, Critical Theory, the goal of which according to William S. Lind 'was not truth but praxis, or revolutionary action: bringing the current society and culture down through unremitting, destructive criticism.[3]

The main aim of the neo-Marxists and Critical Theory is enshrined in this idea:

To Reject the Notion of Objectivity in Knowledge.

This concept posits that knowledge is subjective, influenced by personal feelings, tastes, or opinions. In this theory there is no such thing as absolute truth. The relativism evident in our society today – what's true for you is not true for me – has its seeds in the 1920s with Critical Theory. It rejected, and still does reject, absolute truth in general and Biblical truth in particular.

To develop these ideas and move beyond purely economic and political solutions, Marxists needed input from other disciplines. They delved into sociology and psychology and integrated these fields to fortify their plan.

Maltz further elaborates:

Under this new leadership, the Frankfurt School was to move away from academic concerns to a wider remit, critical social research, which involved an integration of the social sciences, a significant development. Key academics brought in to follow this path were Eric Fromm, the psychoanalyst, Theodor Adorno, the sociologist, and Herbert Marcuse, who we met a little earlier. Things were now going to get a little tasty. Fromm worked with Horkheimer on finding connections between the theories of Marx and Sigmund Freud. The area of attack here was social change and, in particular, the role of the family in society. These men were arrogantly going to interfere with a system that has worked perfectly well since God gave it to mankind as a gift.[4]

Newspeak

Marcuse worked on ways to bring about change breaking established meanings and weaponising language for coercion and oppression.

The Frankfurt School also incorporated the ideas of Wilhelm Reich who contributed by writing about sexual repression. The term 'The Sexual Revolution' used in the 1960s comes from the title of one of his books published 1936.

In 1933, due to the rise of Nazism and many at the School being Jewish, the founders decided to move out of Germany. They went first to Geneva and then, in 1935, to the US. Their plan to influence the Western world subtly took shape, spurred by concerns of fascism resurfacing in the US post-WWII.

Their American friends, particularly Jewish groups, funded the publication of their books from the mid-1950s onward. Adorno and Marcuse, two intelligent German Jews, emerged as trusted figures, teaching how to detect early signs of fascism and prevent its resurgence.

The neo-Marxists targeted three areas: academia, mainstream media, and Hollywood, shaping Western culture for decades. You may be thinking that this report is a conspiracy theory. You may have been advised that when you hear this kind of thing you should regard it as such. The forms of media telling you those things are telling you because they are the real conspiracy. They are the avenues through which these ideas were going to be propagated – and still are.

While there's debate on whether neo-Marxists had a written manifesto, their strategy to subvert Western society is evident in their books and lectures. Like Alice Bailey (see section on the New Age movement), they focused on influencing younger generations, emphasising the long-term nature of their revolution. Lenin once said: "Give me just one generation of youth, and I will change the world."

'The long march through the institutions' is a quote you often encounter in studies of this subject. It is a reference to Mao Zedong's Long March to eventual victory in the Chinese Civil War.

The neo-Marxists began their march in the 1950s firstly through Theodor Adorno's book, *The Authoritarian Personality*.[5] In it, Adorno proposes The Fascism Scale or the F-Scale. By interviewing various groups of people, he created a list of signs to look for that would be used to determine whether someone is going to become a Fascist. He posited that the person who grows up with a traditional Judaeo-Christian background would be the one most likely to show signs of fascism as they age. By using Freudian theory, he placed the suggestion into people's heads, into their subconscious, and therefore into the culture, that Christianity is a big part of the problems in society.

Then Herbert Marcuse comes into the picture. In 1955 he

wrote *Eros and Civilisation*.[6] In it he also pushes the same ideas about fascism but in this case, it's set within the subject of sexuality. He postulates that if you are a monogamist, with a traditional family background you are highly likely to become Fascist. And he goes further by saying that the only way to make sure that you are free of any Fascistic tendencies is to give up any sexual restraints. He promoted polyamory (have as many lovers as you want) and get into as many perversions as you want. That will free you, he said, and make sure you neutralise any Fascistic tendencies.

The next few years were perfect for the propagation of Marcuse's ideas. He was the architect of the alternative society of the 1960s. '*Make Love Not War*' was his slogan and not that of some anonymous bearded hippy.

He became an influential manipulator. Aiming his ideology at the young people of a prosperous US he told them to revolt against their unimaginative families and turn their backs on the traditional structures. His writings proposed having sex with as many people as you like. This would free individuals and make them better people.

He had some unexpected and powerful associates helping the campaign: the free use and popularity of hallucinogenic drugs, and The Pill.

In 1964 Marcuse wrote *One-Dimensional Man*,[7] a marathon rant against the Consumer Society. He announced that we in the West we are 'one-dimensional' because we are being manipulated by the capitalists. This struck a chord at the time, not just with the hippie types where you might expect to find consensus, but in the wider society and even among Christians.

This is what was so clever about the methods of the Frankfurt School. They would identify a problem – and we would agree that rampant consumerism is not beneficial for society – but their answer was not in moderating it. His solution was: revolt against it!

The Italian neo-Marxist, Antonio Gramsci, gave more impetus to these ideas by the proposed use of 'hegemony'. This is the process whereby a dominant class could exert and maintain its influence over people through non-coercive means. He, like the earlier neo-Marxists, suggested that schools, the media, and marketing should be targeted.

Tinker again:

The aim was to get people to think and especially feel for themselves that certain values and practices, such as same-sex marriage, are 'obvious', 'common sense', 'fair' or even 'natural'. Gramsci's vision was to undermine and eventually take over the 'commanding heights of culture'.[8]

As I learned about these things I was taken back to my own youth and recalled how things changed during that time. I began to see what was behind all the rebellion and the promiscuity that I had been involved in during the 1960s and 70s. It happened very slowly and incrementally over decades.

In the years after becoming a Christian I would often hear, in the churches, the 'frog in the pan' illustration. It was said that the devil was manipulating people and organisations to change society and it was like putting a frog in a pan of hot water. If you did this too suddenly the frog would immediately jump out. But if you put the frog in lukewarm water and very slowly heated it then the frog would fall asleep and eventually die by being boiled to death.

This picture was used to show how the enemy worked very subtly over a long period so that people did not notice or object to the changes taking place. As time passed this concept seems to have been forgotten or ridiculed. But here in 2018 finding this ploy was still ongoing just as subtly, just as intentionally and just as effectively, was surprising.

I checked out the symposium event in London that I had seen on TV in the late 60s (mentioned in chapter 1) and confirmed it was indeed Herbert Marcuse who had visited the Roundhouse, one of the venues that were part of the sub-culture then. His books were the ones we discussed in our pub debates at that time. He and others like him were the dominant thinkers. They had the knowledge and were those we relied on to lead society.

Everything mysteriously came together to make the 1960s happen in the way it did. I remembered how the 1967 'Summer of Love' was followed by the year of student protests some of them very violent. I saw how it was a completely fake decade and discovered that Marcuse was one of the instigators. This is verifiable. You can buy books and you can watch videos of Marcuse in action to study the history of these events. I experienced them first-hand, but I did not realise, until recent years, what the driving forces were behind them.

In 1968 the student protests spread from the US to Europe. France was almost brought down by what happened in Paris that year. Nearly every capitol city across Europe had protests as Marcuse was invited to speak in them. Footage captures him giving speeches across the continent. A demonstration in Rome featured a placard reading "Marx, Mao, Marcuse" symbolising the students' allegiance to the intellectual figures Karl Marx, Mao Tse Tung and Herbert Marcuse. This highlighted his significant influence despite his low-profile approach.

From that movement came the emergence of what we now call the New Left.

Maltz explains:

The 'Old Left' were the original political left wing in the West, such as The Labour Party in the UK. They were typified mainly by the blue-collar workers, the working class, who just wanted a fair wage and food on the table. Out of this movement came the Welfare State in the UK after the Second World War. In general terms their politics didn't travel further than a mutual concern for working people wherever they may be. This is the Labour party of Keir Hardie, Harold Wilson and Denis Healey and others. Safe, comfortable and traditionally British.[9]

But it didn't stay safe. We witnessed how Cultural Marxism had its effect in the UK with the rise to power of Ken Livingstone dubbed 'Red Ken', the Labour Leader of the 1970s, and Derek Hatton, a member of a Trotskyist Militant Group who became Deputy Leader of Liverpool City Council in the 1980s.

The New Left concentrated on things like Protest, Liberation, and Identity. Following another of Marcuse's books - *An Essay on Liberation* - young activists and revolutionaries spawned a profusion of protest groups. Animal Liberation, Women's Liberation, the Palestine Liberation Organisation (PLO) and the Gay Liberation movement. Where did they all come from? They all came out of Marxism.

Where did all this lead? One of the main aims of Cultural Marxism eventually became clear: to develop what we now experience as a 'victim culture'. Society was exposed to a whole series of worthy causes that we could become a part of. Victim groups featured black people, women, gay and transgender people, those affected by colonialism and, more recently, those who might in the future be affected by climate change.

Please note that I am not suggesting we judge those caught up in this degenerate mindset. The victims are simply pawns in a global game. The victim groups are not there for the victims. Take the transgender movement for example. It's not about helping those who are confused sexually. It is about the agenda of others who are manipulating the situation to make that issue into something that will divide and conquer. As Christians, we must speak out against the system rather than the individuals caught up in it.

This begs the question: who and where are the Cultural Marxists pushing this ideological agenda? I can't say for sure but there may be many liberal or left-leaning university professors or social commentators who fit this bill.

I want to note that I am not being political here. I am not pro-right wing or pro-left wing or promoting any other political ideas. This is a spiritual issue. The devil is behind it, and he will use any means he can to achieve his aims.

To understand this, at a deeper level – i.e., to see where the world is going with this – we must look back, for a moment, to one historic event.

Babel.

The Ominous Tower

After the Flood, God gave Noah certain commands and made a covenant with him and with the earth (Gen. 9:1-17). He wanted

Noah and his sons to spread out, multiply and replenish the earth. But man had other plans:

Now the whole earth had one language and the same words. And as people migrated from the east, they found a plain in the land of Shinar and settled there. And they said to one another, 'Come, let us make bricks, and burn them thoroughly.' And they had brick for stone, and bitumen for mortar. Then they said, 'Come, let us build ourselves a city and a tower with its top in the heavens, and let us make a name for ourselves, lest we be dispersed over the face of the whole earth.' (Genesis 11: 1-4)

Understand the global nature of this. Tinker again:

God's cultural mandate to 'fill the earth and subdue it' is given to human beings in Genesis 1:28 and reiterated to Noah in Genesis 9:7. This is roundly repudiated by the peoples of the earth in Genesis 11:4 as they decide to settle on the plain of Shinar to build a tower so that they would <u>not</u> be scattered over the globe.[10]

This account makes it clear that rebellion was at the heart of Babel: Let's all work together to form a global system to throw off God's restraints. And that is what Cultural Marxism is all about – it's the same spirit. The aim of Cultural Marxism, as was (classical) Marxism, is rebellion leading eventually to totalitarianism. The state controlling all the people. The reason I say that I'm not being political is because whatever political persuasion you might be will not make any difference in the coming scenario. We may identify some groups as far right and others as far left – but there will be no right and left in the future scenario.

When rebellion results in chaos a small number will come to the fore and provide a solution to the world's problems. A small group – and ultimately one man – controlling a globalist society. It's about control and diminishing freedoms.

In the west 'marginalised' groups are turning the tables on anyone who disagrees with their supposed plight.

But it is clear, in the neo-Marxist view, with the ever-expanding number of victim groups, no Christian can ever be regarded as a victim.

Examples of Critical Theory

Tinker describes Bulverism, a term coined by C. S. Lewis:

... whereby an objector's belief is assumed to be wrong because of bias and can then therefore be discounted. The reasons for one's objections do not then need to be considered.

And as he points out:

In fact it is to neo-Marxism's advantage that one does not draw people's attention to reasons, for then their own position might be examined and found wanting while the alternative position is found strong and compelling.[11]

So, what is being said here is: If you don't agree it is because you are a fascist and there can be no free speech for fascists. This is a sign of the collapsing culture of the West. Let us look at some evidence of it.

In November 2020, Richard Page, a magistrate and NHS Trust non-executive director, was removed from his positions for expressing his belief, during an adoption case discussion, in the importance of placing children with a mother and a father whenever possible.[12]

In the same year, Kristie Higgs, a mother of two, lost her job as a secondary school pastoral assistant for sharing concerns about age-inappropriate themes in Relationships and Sex Education (RSE) lessons.[13]

Mary Douglas, a Conservative councillor in Salisbury for nearly 15 years, was ousted in November 2019 for opposing the use of public funds for a Pride event.[14]

In February 2018, I purchased a ticket for the premiere screening of the film *'Voices of the Silenced'*[15] at Vue Cinema, Piccadilly, London. This documentary features 15 individuals' stories about moving away from or successfully overcoming same-sex attraction and related behaviours. LGBTQ+ activists pressured the cinema to cancel the screening, despite a prior agreement. Instead of watching the film, I joined a group outside the cinema protesting about the suppression of free speech. The cinema, fearing hostile actions by LGBTQ+ groups, stood firm in its decision. The film challenges the notion that people are prisoners of their sexuality. It highlights the voices of those who've moved away from same-sex desires but are silenced by mainstream media, marginalised, and targeted by LGBTQ+ activists and legislation. The organisation that produced the documentary had its bank accounts closed following campaigns initiated by LGBTQ+ activists.[16]

In November 2018, Izzy Montague faced victimisation after raising concerns about her son's primary school promoting LGBTQ+ issues to young children. Her 4-year-old was compelled to participate in a 'Gay Pride' event with no opt-outs allowed.

When Izzy met with the school's executive headteacher to discuss her complaint, she faced hostility. She was warned that expressing views perceived as racist, homophobic, or transphobic would lead to the meeting's termination.

The Hate Police
The Scottish Government and the Scottish Police, under the banner 'One Scotland,' ran a hate crime awareness campaign that primarily featured posters addressing 'Bigots,' 'homophobes,' 'transphobes,' and others, signed 'Yours, Scotland.'

While the goal of reducing hate in Scotland is admirable, there are serious concerns with the campaign. What exactly constitutes a 'hate crime,' and is there a significant difference between a 'crime' and a 'hate crime'? Aren't all crimes crimes? One of the most controversial posters read: "Dear Bigots, you can't spread your religious hate here. End of sermon. Yours, Scotland." But what exactly is a 'bigot'?

The dictionary definition is "a person who is intolerant towards those holding different opinions". This is a good definition, provided we agree on what intolerance means. The problem is that if someone is very convinced of their own opinion and of the wrongness of other opinions, this can be perceived as intolerance of those holding other opinions ...

The implication is that all religious people are bigots. This is insulting, but it is hard to believe that the insult is not intentional in this.[17]

These are all clear examples of Bulverism.

Where is it All Leading?

Many consider these changes as progress, much like I did in the 1970s when I opposed those I saw as hindering "improvements" in society. However, today's progressives are unforgiving. Western culture – built on Judaeo-Christian principles – is becoming subordinate to political correctness while most of the population, apparently unaware of what is happening, remain unperturbed.

In Luke 17, when questioned about the arrival of the kingdom of God, Jesus didn't attribute its coming to the achievements of believers but stated it would follow his return. He detailed the spiritual and social conditions preceding this event. Concerning spiritual aspects, he cautioned about the rise of false prophets and messiahs.

In addressing social aspects, he referenced the times of Noah and Lot. Despite living in unrighteous eras, Noah and Lot, righteous men, faced widespread wickedness. In Noah's time, God said he regretted creating humanity (see Genesis 6:5-8), and in Lot's day, God was distressed by the sin and sexual perversion (see Genesis 18:16 – 19:38).

Jesus predicted a similar cultural backdrop just before his return – a proliferation of evil, wickedness, and immorality. Despite this, life will continue seemingly unaffected, with people tolerating and even celebrating the prevailing decadence. They will engage in everyday activities like dining out, forming relationships, marrying, building, and making future plans, displaying a desensitisation to the surrounding culture of evil.

The concept of 'sin' is rarely used today, both in society and the church. The Christian view of sin and how we deal with it is a crucial part of our relationship with God. We have fallen nature and are sinful beings. What sin we commit is ultimately against our creator God. But redefined by Cultural Marxists, the only sin in our culture is opposing victim groups or individuals within them. This is the path society has taken and yet no one knows who is controlling it! It seems that everyone is bowing down to the new god of tolerance and inclusion.

According to Lenin – founder of the Russian Communist Party, leader of the 1917 Revolution, architect, builder, and first head of the Soviet state – destruction requires two elements: a small group of vanguard thinkers who are convinced they know better than everyone else, and a much larger group of fellow travellers who don't really understand the vanguard's endgame. The people Lenin termed "useful idiots".

The Church is seriously affected by this path that society is on but remains mostly silent. Church leaders may not be speaking out for fear they appear politically biased and potentially losing congregants. However, these are spiritual, not political issues. The lack of awareness and understanding among church leaders is evident in their silence.

Over my lifetime, I've seen Communist ideology infiltrate many nations. Marxists, often Russian, infiltrate a country, forming groups to stir up discontent with that country's government. As support for their cause grows, violent revolution follows. This was the West's fear from the late 1940s onwards, leading to what became known as the Cold War. The growing anxiety among Western nations, encapsulated in the "Domino Theory," posited that as countries fell to Communist ideology, others would follow. This happened in China, Vietnam, Korea, Cuba, and other parts of the world. It continues today, often involving war and bloodshed, although sometimes the overthrow focuses more on the cultural aspects of a nation. I believe this is the root of much of the anti-colonialism we see in the West today.

There is a need to recognise the subtler form of Marxism eroding Western culture. It is a pervasive force demanding a vigilant response from the Church and its members. It is the root cause and means by which Christians will face increasing persecution, making it imperative to understand it. What we now call Socialism has been, in the past, a diluted form of Marxism but is now becoming increasingly like the deadly concentrated type.

A Summary of this Research

In summary, we've explored how Classical Marxism was repackaged in the West, consistently urging rebellion against the status quo without proposing solutions. This has given rise to postmodernism and the resultant Political Correctness, which increasingly oppresses our faith and Judaeo-Christian foundations.

My investigations also delved into the deeper issue of humanity's belief that it can achieve things without God, as seen in the story of Babel.

We saw how society – and to some extent, the church – has become desensitised to sin and has not recognised the signs of impending judgement.

Lastly, we've highlighted the apparent ignorance or lack of understanding within churches regarding the detrimental effects of Cultural Marxism on society. The accompanying silence may be attributed to a fear of political bias, but also shows a lack of recognition of its spiritual roots.

Notes:

[1] https://en.wikipedia.org/wiki/Frankfurt_School

[2] Maltz, S. (2018), *Noise: A Search for Sense*, Ilford, Saffron Planet Publishing, p11.

[3] Tinker, M. (2018), *That Hideous Strength: How the West was Lost*, Welwyn Garden City, EP Books, p 51.

[4] Maltz, S. (2018), *Into the Lion's Den: Reaching a World gone Mad*, Ilford, Saffron Planet Publishing, p22.

[5] Adorno, T., Frenkel-Brunswick, E., Levinson, D., Sanford, R. (1969), *The Authoritarian Personality*, New York, Norton & Company.

[6] Marcuse, H. (1969), *Eros and Civilisation*, London, Sphere Books.

[7] Marcuse, H. (1964), *One-dimensional Man*, London, Routledge.

[8] Tinker, M. (2019), *Wet, Woke archbishop completes the march through the institutions*, in *The Conservative Woman* online magazine at: https://www.conservativewoman.co.uk

[9] Maltz, S. (2018), *Noise: A Search for Sense*, Ilford, Saffron Planet Publishing, p19.

[10] Tinker, M. (2018), *That Hideous Strength: How the West was Lost*, Welwyn Garden City, EP Books, p37 - p38.

[11] Ibid, p56

[12] See: https://christianconcern.com/cccases/richard-page/ last accessed 12.11.20.

[13] The story in The Telegraph: https://www.telegraph.co.uk/news/2020/09/21/school-employee-sacked-sharing-petition-lgbt-lessons-says-parents/

[14] See: https://christianconcern.com/cccases/mary-douglas/

[15] See: www.voicesof the silenced.com

[16] See: https://christianconcern.com/news/christian-ministry-harassed-and-facing-bank-account-closure/ Last accessed 12.11.20.

[17] See: https://christianconcern.com/comment/scotlands-alarming-hate-posters/ Last accessed 09.02.21.

Appendix 3

READING LISTS AND OTHER RESOURCES

Books

Recommended reading beyond those mentioned in the footnotes:

To Life! Rediscovering Biblical Church, Steve Maltz, Saffron Planet, 2008.

Rees Howells, *Intercessor*, Norman Grubb, Lutterworth, 2003.

How the Church Lost the Way, Steve Maltz, Saffron Planet, 2009.

Prophecy Past and Present, Clifford Hill, Eagle Publishing, Guildford, 1989.

Dynamic Prayer: Communicating with God, David Noakes, Sovereign World Ltd., 2011.

Listening with Understanding, Clifford Hill, Sovereign World Ltd., 2011.

The Left's Jewish Problem: Jeremy Corbyn, Israel and Antisemitism, Dave Rich, Biteback Publishing Ltd., 2018.

Unbreakable Love: The Love of God in the Message of the Prophets, Clifford Hill, Centre for Contemporary Ministry, 2010.

Living in Babylon, Clifford Hill and Monica Hill, Handsel Press, 2016.

DVDs

Many of these can now be found online as digital resources.

Jerusalem: The Covenant City, Hatikvah Films, 2015.

Whose Land? – Parts 1 and 2. A 2-part documentary film by historians and international lawyers challenging the claims that the Jewish people have no historical ties to Jerusalem and that the Jewish presence in Jerusalem is illegal. Alarmingly, this perspective has gained traction in the Western world. Available at: www.titledeedmedia.com.

Websites for Further Research

Fellowship of Israel Related Ministries: https://firmisrael.org
Intercessors for Israel: https://www.ifi.org.il

The Tishrei Bible School (exploring the Hebraic roots of the Bible) and The Cedars School of Biblical Family Life: www.tishrei.org

Ebenezer Operation Exodus: https://ebenezer-oe.org

Prophecy Today UK: https://prophecytoday.uk

C & M Heritage: www.candmministries.org.uk

The International Mission to Jewish People: www.imjp.org

Organisations Providing Support

For those struggling with ungodly and/or unbiblical church practices and teaching:

Issachar Ministries: Visit issacharministries.co.uk and click on the 'Outside In' link, or email outsidein@issacharministries. co.uk, or write to Issachar Ministries UK, Bedford Heights, Brickhill Drive, Bedford, MK41 7PH.

Village Link: For those in rural communities, visit https:// villagelink.substack.com or write to: Village Hope, Prior's Frome Chapel, Prior's Frome, Hereford, HR1 4EP.

IMUK Sunday Gatherings: An international online community at issacharministries.co.uk or write to Issachar Ministries UK, Bedford Heights address above.

Followers of the Way at: http://www.vfjuk.org.uk/FOTW/

Living Word Church Network UK. Email: admin@lwcn.uk

Becoming a Christian, Sharing the Gospel

Evangelism Explosion: Learn to understand and present the gospel message. Visit https://evangelismexplosion.org/resources/ and read/download their 'digital tract' which explains the Gospel for unbelievers and serves as an evangelism tool.

Research Papers, Articles, and Leaflets

My Enthusiasm for 'New Church': A series of articles available at anthonywhelan.net under the heading *"Disillusionment: A Door to Freedom"*.

Ungodly Laws Leaflet: Ungodly Laws Passed in Britain Since 1950, Issachar Ministries Trust, 2014. Available on the C&MM website at www.candmministries.org.uk or by messging: contact@anthonywhelan.net

The Repentance and Intercession Leaflets: Issachar Ministries Trust, 2014. Available on the C&MM website at www.candmministries.org.uk or by messging: contact@anthonywhelan.net

The Land Promised: An article about the references in the Bible to the land that God gave to the offspring of Abraham, Isaac and Jacob, (includes actual references), available at www.anthonywhelan.net

Will there be a 'Rapture' of the Church?

Some believe there will be a rapture—a snatching away—of believers to heaven before the Tribulation, which, according to a reading of the prophecies of Daniel, will last for seven years.

This is the 'pre-tribulation' rapture view. It holds that believers will escape the Tribulation, which will be the outpouring of the Lord's wrath and judgements upon the earth against evil.

Others hold to a 'post-tribulation' rapture view, asserting that believers will live through the final seven years before the return of the Lord and must be prepared to suffer. If this view is held then it contradicts various scriptures, and Jesus's own words, which state that we will not know the day or the hour when He will return. The seven-year period is clearly laid out in scripture with starting, intermediate, and finish events.

There are many scriptures which support a rapture view and believers who earnestly study the end-times adopt one or the other of these views. Meanwhile, some leaders in new church streams ridicule the idea of any kind of rapture, possibly because they believe the Church will overcome all earthly difficulties.

Proponents of the post-tribulation rapture sometimes accuse pre-tribulation believers of being escapist and indifferent to the suffering of others. Pre-tribulation believers counter that we must be ready for the imminent return of the Lord, as Jesus himself indicated. If the post-tribulation believers are correct, then we know He won't appear today, because we haven't yet experienced the tribulation, which, according to Daniel 9:27, will begin with a treaty or covenant made by the anti-Christ.

The sequence of events in scripture is not laid out in an easy-to-understand way, so we must examine many different passages before drawing our own conclusions. Daniel did say that the words of his prophecy would be sealed until the time of the end, and I believe these scriptures are now being unveiled to those who have eyes to see.

Until I have thoroughly studied the scriptures, I will adopt the position that we need to be ready for Him at any time. This way, I lose nothing. It is better to be proved wrong about the timing and live in readiness, than to be found unprepared.

Milton Keynes UK
Ingram Content Group UK Ltd.
UKHW050809181124
2908UKWH00069B/779